Show Your Work

THE PAYOFFS AND HOW-TO'S OF WORKING OUT LOUD

JANE BOZARTH

WILEY

Published by Wiley

One Montgomery Street, Suite 1200, San Francisco, CA 94104-4594

www.wiley.com

Cover image: Shutterstock

Cover design: Faceout Studio

For additional copies or bulk purchases of this book or to learn more about Wiley's Workplace Learning offerings, please contact us toll free at 1-866-888-5159 or by email at workplacelearning@wiley.com.

Wiley also publishes its books in a variety of electronic formats and by print-on-demand. Some material included with standard print versions of this book may not be included in e-books or in print-on-demand. If the version of this book that you purchased references media such as a CD or DVD that was not included in your purchase, you may download this material at http://booksupport.wiley.com. For more information about Wiley products, visit www.wiley.com.

Library of Congress Cataloging-in-Publication Data has been applied for and is on file with the Library of Congress.
ISBN 978-1-118-86362-6 (pbk); ISBN 978-1-118-86401-2 (ebk); ISBN 978-1-118-86350-3 (ebk)

Printed in the United States of America

FIRST EDITION

PB Printing   10 9 8 7 6 5 4 3 2 1

Contents

1   Introduction

12   Benefits to Organizations

30   Workers: What's In It For You?

50   What Is Knowledge? and Why Do People Share It?

58   "This Is How I Do That."

118   Learning & Development

136   How?

180   Index

"Anyone who's diligently followed a written recipe only to have a terrible end result has felt the disconnect between tacit and explicit knowledge."

Introduction

"Everybody works. They create documents and presentations. They schedule and attend events. They comment on other people's work."

~ **John Stepper,** johnstepper.com

CALL IT WHAT YOU LIKE

When you were a kid, you likely had a math teacher or two who insisted that you "show your work." It enabled him or her to see how you arrived at a final answer, what kind of thinking or steps got you there—and where you might have made a mistake. You can think of showing your work in any terms you'd like. Some call it "working out loud," making work visible, making work discoverable, or narrating work. There are any number of approaches to showing work, from writing to talking to drawing to photographing and more. And now, with so many new, often free tools people like to use, it's easier than ever before.

Showing Your Work Benefits Everyone

In its simplest, most obvious benefit, showing work helps an idea connect with someone else who needs it. The woman in Kansas who finds a YouTube video that helps her change the windshield wipers on her car. The man in London who, in a colleague's blog post, finds an answer to a bedeviling question. In organizations, it makes the walls between silos more permeable, helping talent pools connect and saving workers countless hours in looking for information.

While we're good at documenting standards, most of what we need to know is exception handling—what we must know and do and respond to that's outside a schematic or process plan or SOP. John Hagel and John Seeley Brown assert that "as much as two-thirds of headcount time in major enterprise functions like marketing, manufacturing, and supply chain management is spent on exception handling." (http://blogs.hbr.org/2010/09/social-software/). My own favorite neighborhood handyman, Mike, has never been here when he did not encounter an exception: the hole the builder cut for the attic stairs is not the standard size for the home repair store stairs Mike came to install; a repair to the porch railing found that the "standard" rails the builder used are no longer in stock, and on and on. Showing our work helps make what we do more visible and discoverable—particularly in the area of exception handling—and helps to record the information for future use.

The Silo Problem

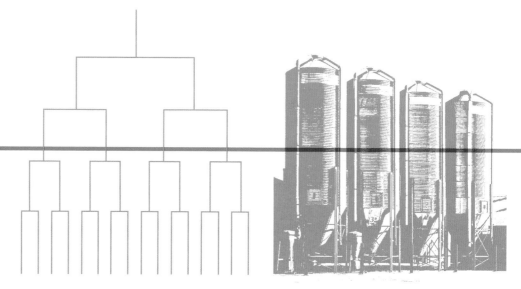

Information flows up and down vertical chain of command

Looking very much like what we otherwise call "silos"

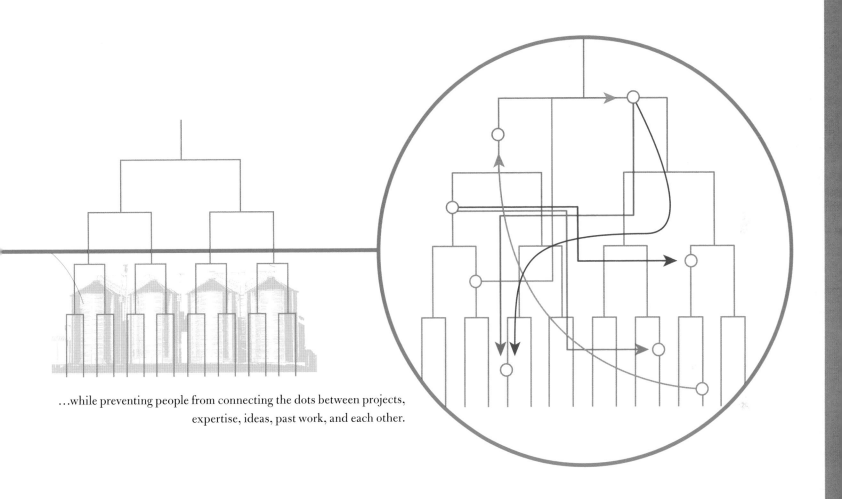

...while preventing people from connecting the dots between projects, expertise, ideas, past work, and each other.

"If your dots are not observable/visible/transparent, then it's impossible to connect them."

~BRIAN TULLIS

The Documentation Problem

Harold Jarche has written extensively on personal knowledge management, particularly the problem with documentation: while it's fairly easy to codify things like events and outputs, the tacit, implicit knowledge that is part and parcel of things like decisions is much harder to capture.

The attempt to reduce complexity to simplicity is fine when you're refining the bones of a production process. It's not fine when you assert that "leadership" is a matter of following four simple steps.

And sooner or later, documentation always breaks down. In the desire to oversimplify we end up with documents that are akin to having a map without landmarks or road signs, with the organization unable to see the routes people really take. (Brown & Duguid, 1990). We know what to do but not how it gets done. We need better maps.

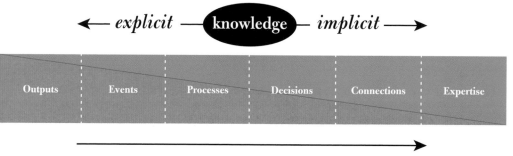

Codifying Knowledge

←— *explicit* —— **knowledge** —*implicit* —→

| Outputs | Events | Processes | Decisions | Connections | Expertise |

Increased difficulty to codify and share

Thanks to Harold Jarche
jarche.com

SHOWING YOUR WORK ISN'T NEW

A thousand years ago a wanderer who drew a map at journey's end might be described as someone who "showed their work." Apprenticeship in many ways offered a "show your work" approach, with the inclusion of instruction and feedback. Electronic tools introduced in the late 20th century made showing work much easier, as many of this book's examples will show.

SHOWING YOUR WORK ISN'T MYSTICAL

One of the problems with the literature on showing work is that much of it is just too abstract and conceptual, with complex models and illustrations with maps and loops and actors. While the models may in some ways be accurate, and often in good intentions reflect the creators' enthusiasm, they don't seem to be very *useful*, else more

people would be using them. They can also be daunting to the already-busy knowledge worker and the guy who fixes copy machines who works from his car most of the day.

As with the problem of "best practices," which are really only best in their original context, the problem with models and formulas is that they often fit common circumstances in only the most abstract way. We see a similar issue with traditional ideas of "knowledge management" (KM), offering things like manufacturing schematics that look great on paper but don't reveal stumbling points, exceptions, or extenuating circumstances. They don't account for what can happen due to group dynamics, overengaged process owners, and business owners who need to be educated. Likewise, asking a worker to "just write down everything you do" can get us what, but doesn't capture *how*. We are seduced by the idea that

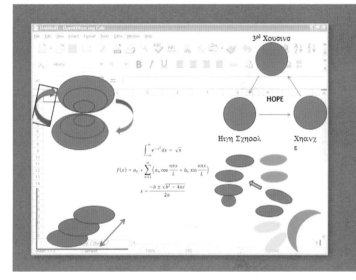

activities like this give us predictability and exact science.

There's also a danger of the formula, or the tool, driving the train. A common criticism of KM is that it attempts to isolate the actor from the work, and the work from context. Sharing work should be an organic activity in everyday workflow, not some separate overengineered process that eventually proves to be nothing but more work.

IT'S NOT JUST FOR "KNOWLEDGE WORKERS"

I have been in the workforce for more than twenty years, mostly in areas like L&D and HR. If one thing has nagged at me for all that time, it is concerns about the segment of the workforce that is, it seems, uniformly marginalized. We focus on the "knowledge worker," typically viewed as a college graduate working in a white collar job, at a desk, maybe at a desk in a cubicle, maybe at a desk in a home office. It's fine to want to know what they know, but what about the rest of the workforce? As noted by Mike Rowe (http://profoundlydisconnected.com/), "No one ever stops to talk to the guys working on the film crew."

You appreciate the hands-on or technical worker when you've tried a home repair a bit beyond your abilities, or despite following all directions failed at gardening. Anyone who's diligently followed a written recipe only to have a terrible end result has felt the disconnect between tacit and explicit knowledge.

Here's an example. Ask an expert to write down her recipe for caramel apples and this is what you'll get:

Caramel Apples

----

6 apples
14-oz package of caramels, unwrapped
2 Tablespoons milk

⊖ **Remove stems from apple; push a craft stick into the top. Butter a baking sheet.**

⊖ **Place caramels and milk in a microwave safe bowl. Microwave 2 minutes, stirring once. Allow to cool briefly.**

⊖ **Roll each apple quickly in caramel sauce until well coated. Place on prepared sheet to set.**

Here's what happens when you ask an expert to show her work. This Snapguide on making caramel apples, from Bridget Burge's *Bridget's Everyday Cooking* (http://snapguide.com/guides/make-caramel-apples-1/) includes some things a novice might not know, and an expert might not think to write down:

Step 2 of 19

Okay so here's the supplies! First things first, wash and dry your apples and then place them in the freezer for about 15 minutes. This helps the caramel set properly on the apples.

Step 3 of 19

Get a microwave safe 4 cup measuring cup. I HIGHLY suggest you use this instead of just a bowl because it's 10X easier to dunk your apples in.

Pour milk into your measuring cup and place in the microwave for one minute.

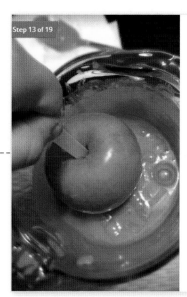

And now its time :)! Simply dunk your apple into the caramel sauce gently turning the apple to allow the caramel to get ALL of the apple.

Take the apples from the freezer, place on a baking sheet lined with parchment paper. It is important you use parchment paper or waxed paper without it your apples will stick and become a mess.

Embracing a "Show Your Work" approach helps to include that segment of the workforce that's so often been marginalized. Also: we can get a better understanding of what the tradesperson or the craftsperson does. How did the groundskeeper create that elephant topiary in front of the children's wing at the local hospital? How did the pastry chef uniformly brown 400 Baked Alaskas to be served simultaneously? It's important, for clear communication, to strip out extraneous information. But sometimes we strip out too much, and the bones we're left with aren't enough. As Brown and Duguid (1991) noted, taking out too much information about the daily reality of the work can leave you holding a map with no landmarks.

NO ONE SAID IT ALL HAD TO BE PUBLIC

As we'll see in the examples, everything doesn't need to be shared everywhere. Proprietary information about a particular client may need to stay within a single work group. Details on fixing a particular water heater might be appropriate only for the company repair people scattered across North America. We don't want people to be deluged with information that is truly relevant only to a few. The problem is, often those making that call don't know who else might benefit. I once got a big work problem solved by a Twitter connection who teaches in China. And another by a consultant who specializes in helping retail and restaurant clients make their environments more comfortable for those with Asperger's and autism. One of the challenges is to figure out where to best share work for maximum benefit to everyone.

NO ONE SAID IT HAD TO BE INSTAGRAM

It seems as soon as people start talking tools there is quickly a hue and cry against Facebook, or LinkedIn, or YouTube. While I see a lot of overcaution (Really? Your dress code and wellness program are secret? Can't have cameras inside the workplace? Not even if it's for a limited, "I need to photograph this cake" use? Ok, not even then? How about drawing? Have they banned drawing, too?) I agree that there need to be guidelines for where to share what. Here's one approach:

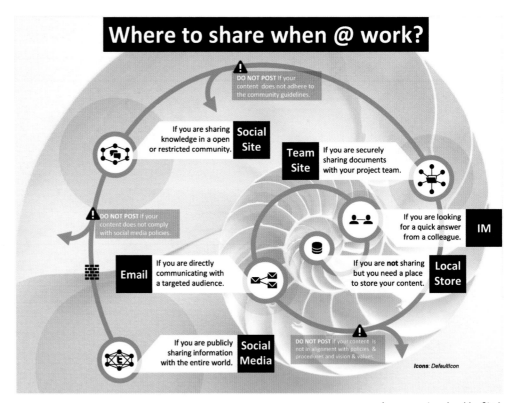

Image courtesy Joachim Stroh

FINALLY: SHOWING YOUR WORK IS NOT ABOUT "INFORMATION"

The quest for "information" generates:

- **Spreadsheets**
- **Meetings**
- **Quotas**
- **TPS reports**
- **Status updates**
- **Top-down dissemination**
- **Sacred story versus real story**
- **Only good news**

"Information" alone is not enough. Adding the better information to more understanding of the exception, the behavior of the individual, the input of the expert, the workaround, the correction, the error helps generate a more robust picture that will help to inform and further refine enacting skillful work.

Remember: Communication over information. Conversation over tools.

So: Let's get going.

Knowing *what* gets done is not the same as knowing *how* it gets done.

Benefits to Organizations

Narrating work offers myriad benefits to organizations, from better locating talent and finding tacit knowledge to increasing efficiencies to improving communication. One of the problems with traditional knowledge management is the temptation to try and oversimplify an unavoidably complex task. Building a house takes much more than a blueprint; a schematic of a manufacturing process may, from 50,000 feet, look like a series of simple steps but on the shop floor be a very different proposition with many moving parts and frequent exceptions.

> *"If everyone in the team narrated their work openly, we wouldn't need any meetings to assess project status and we would gain a lot of time."*

~**JEROEN SANGERS,** http://en.blog.zyncro.com/2013/05/16/working-out-loud/

But they don't tell us the story the person in charge of the process, on the floor, every day, would tell: what to do when a supplier fails to ship a critical component, or a flu epidemic derails schedules, or someone creates a custom shim for an ill-fitting part without telling anyone about the flaw. The problem with documentation? Well . . . the reality is rarely what's documented. So how can showing work help the organization?

INCREASED EFFICIENCIES

- ⮑ Reduction in meetings

- ⮑ Fewer silos and decrease in redundancy

- ⮑ Saved time and energy

- ⮑ Reduction of time spent both in searching for information and people/relationships

- ⮑ Reduction in time spent interpreting historical documents and artifacts

- ⮑ Connecting talent pools

- ⮑ Improvement in creating and storing information and artifacts

- ⮑ Capturing explicit, but not tacit, knowledge

(**Author note:** This does not address the problem of meetings held from dysfunction, like creating intentional delays, discomfort with using newer, more efficient tools, simply liking to "get together" even when it is not productive, and having meetings to give the appearance of working. In other words: sometimes managers don't want to reduce meetings. Interestingly, I have worked in two organizations fueled by "standing meetings," in which allotted time gets filled whether there is anything important to discuss or not. I worked in a third in which there were no standing meetings, and it seemed to get by just fine without them.)

OVERCOMING TRADITIONAL ORGANIZATIONAL COMMUNICATION TRAPS

Many organizations are good at capturing basics of explicit information: to order product Z fill out form N; submit requests by Thursday. But much of our time is spent dealing with Barely Repeatable Processes, the ones that deal with people, and which often are managed through a morass of emails, lunches out, Post-it Notes, and meetings. It is, in other words, how most of us spend most of our days. They are fluid (non-rigid) processes and events with many moving parts that are not easily mapped, as with a manufacturing process.

The truth is, asking someone to "write down everything they know" or "list everything they do" just doesn't work very well. We can find out what they do but not how they get things done. And overengineered, bureaucratized reports and documentation processes are often exercises in futility, as they capture the "what" of work but not the "how."

The image on this page shows an example of a newly implemented process for submitting status reports. It was provided from an HR outsourcing firm middle manager who asked to remain anonymous. The IT department developed it as a way to force employees to use SharePoint instead of the less formal tools workers had been using. When I asked for detail, as the image is not very legible, the person who submitted it said: "You don't want to be able to read it. You'll go blind."

A colleague working with a software group—who also asked to remain anonymous—reports: "When I was working with [A Software Company], the CEO wanted my help formulating this highly replicable process of creating video: gathering info, production planning, shooting, and then editing and post-prod into a simple linear process with a few decision points along the way. Of course, that all worked in theory, but the practical reality was that we were working with all contracted filmmakers, we had international travel issues, timezones, logistical concerns with film storage—you name it.

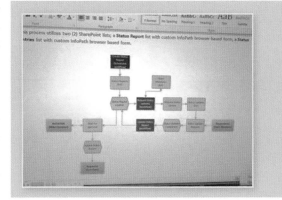

All the things that go along with film-making. She was endlessly frustrated that the artistry of film-making would get lost in the quest to scale and flex her process, and yet she also didn't want to compromise client service/satisfaction in a quest to streamline the people/processes that we *could* control. And there you have it."

BRIAN TULLIS: WHY OBSERVABLE WORK?

Here are some of the things that I worry about for my team and my company. How can we effectively:

1. Share what might be half-baked ideas that would benefit from outside input, but that we don't share openly for fear of being shot down?

2. Document and share lessons learned on projects/audits/operational failures so that we don't repeat the same mistakes again?

3. Narrate our work so that we don't have to drag each other into status meetings and waste our collective time reporting what we did instead of letting status emerge naturally from our visible work?

4. Make our electronic documents come alive and be linked across an organization instead of going to die in networked file shares and content silos?

5. Describe exactly the heck it is we are talking about when it comes to social media being used to get work done without calling it "Wikipedia for the workplace" or "Facebook for the enterprise"?

Translation:

1. Promote and foster innovation

2. Promote best practices and continuous improvement

3. Narrate our work and expose it through targeted activity streams

4. Unlock our documents and leverage hypertext

5. Make it all happen without coming across to our colleagues as social-media-hyping, jargon-spewing-idiots

My personal reasons for believing that these are important come from my own core values that I share with anyone that will listen:

⤷ Transparency

⤷ Continuous improvement and learning

⤷ Narrating what I do because it helps me get work done, and hopefully helps others too

⤷ Debate and disagreement as a means for seeking truth

⤷ Exposing failures so that they are a lesson for others

http://nextthingsnext.blogspot.com/2010/09/gathering-my-thoughts-on-observable.html

THE PROBLEM OF UNDERSHARING

Liz Guthridge writes about the problems old-school, Tayloristic views of workplace communication continue to perpetuate. The practices constrain workers who need to work with external clients and customers, perpetuate a sense of distrust between workers and management, slow problem resolution, defeat goals of being "agile," and hamstring workers so that they cannot contribute in meaningful ways. Some of the old behaviors are:

⊖ Sharing information on a "need-to-know basis" to protect corporate secrets

⊖ Withholding information as a way to maintain efficiency

⊖ Avoiding saying anything so as not to worry people

⊖ Staying silent to avoid acknowledging a problem that doesn't yet have a solution

⊖ Sugarcoating information to try to put a positive spin on negative situations

⊖ Saving time (especially leaders' time) by staying quiet

⊖ Keeping information under wraps as a power play

http://connectconsultinggroup.com/avoid-undersharing-at-work/
Thanks to Liz Guthridge, Connect Consulting

LEARNING FROM MISTAKES

We learn so much the hard way, but are rewarded for our successes and often punished for even minor or inconsequential failures; what is learned this way is often swept under the rug. But there can be so much to learn from exploring someone else's mistakes, especially if we can get insight into what caused them and how they were corrected. U.S. National Teacher of the Year Sarah Brown Wessling offers her own example of a devoted practitioner working to improve both her own practice and that of others, sometimes stumbling along the way. This is available as a long, in-depth video; please watch it when you have a chance. See https://www.teachingchannel.org/videos/when-lesson-plans-fail .

While her class on *The Crucible* was being taped, Wessling realized her lesson plan was going terribly awry. It happened that she was being videotaped that day; she went back and narrated the video, describing what went wrong and how she fixed it. Then she uploaded it to the Teaching Channel site so others could learn from it.

In class that day Wessling handed out what she felt was a straightforward assignment. But the teenage students were confused and grew increasingly loud and disgruntled. Wessling notes it would be easy to write that off to problems with listening or disrespect, but instead says, "I choose to see it this way: I've done something to make them act like this, because they usually don't. I realized I had completely misfired. I didn't create enough scaffolds for them to be successful . . . [in the end] I didn't teach them anything."

Wessling had 5 minutes to adjust her plan before the next class started. "What I learned from the first class is that this was too hard," which prompted her to revisit her goals for the lesson and the big ideas she was trying to convey. She then describes what went through her mind as she reshaped the lesson even as students in the upcoming class were settling into their seats. This proves a fascinating narration of the tacit, hard-to-capture process known as "thinking on your feet."

She then discusses the experience with fellow teacher Kate, because "these things are hard to process on your own." Wessling comments that developing a trusted network, with people who can help you think things through and give honest feedback, is vital to successful practice. But Wessling did more. Rather than just bury the conversation with her colleague as part of her day, Wessling captured it, too, and included it in the video she shared.

Wessling did not set out to "work out loud" that day. But by narrating what happened she was able to tie the events to a larger conversation about the struggle to meet the needs of adults working with Common Core education standards, and the kids who needed to learn.

She ends her commentary with a reflection on the bigger picture of what she learned from the experience, the need to adhere to standards in a way that "makes sense to the kids in front of us."

The question: Which would be more useful to the novice: An out-of-context 6-minute video of Sarah's perfect final lesson, or the longer version showing how it evolved and why she made her final design choices?

In considering the value Wessling's very public reflection can bring, think about the support it has: a confident practitioner, secure enough to admit she makes mistakes; an ability to recognize when something is going wrong and working to identify the root cause rather than lay easy blame (in this case, on the kids); and an administrative structure and work culture that tolerates those mistakes and sees them as opportunities to improve. Wessling's mistake was unfortunate, but it was not the end of the world. What do more workplaces need to do to allow public reflection on ways to get better? What cultural elements currently in place support or inhibit free conversation?

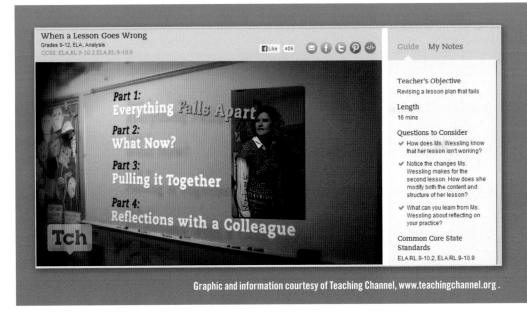

When a Lesson Goes Wrong
Grades 9-12, ELA, Analysis
CCSS: ELA.RL.9-10.2, ELA.RL.9-10.9

Like 409

Guide   My Notes

Part 1:
Everything Falls Apart

Part 2:
What Now?

Part 3:
Pulling it Together

Part 4:
Reflections with a Colleague

Tch

Teacher's Objective
Revising a lesson plan that fails

Length
16 mins

Questions to Consider
✔ How does Ms. Wessling know that her lesson isn't working?
✔ Notice the changes Ms. Wessling makes for the second lesson. How does she modify both the content and structure of her lesson?
✔ What can you learn from Ms. Wessling about reflecting on your practice?

Common Core State Standards
ELA.RL.9-10.2, ELA.RL.9-10.9

Graphic and information courtesy of Teaching Channel, www.teachingchannel.org.

Note, too, the prompts shown on the Teaching Channel's interface, with questions to encourage the viewer's reflection and application to practice.

Many of us have ideas that don't match reality. Here's a project postmortem from an anonymous gamer. It turns out an idea for a game is not the same as the reality of developing that game, and the programmer's point of view is very different from the designer's. This bit of after-the-fact reflection offers valuable from-the-trenches insight into something that might save someone else from learning the hard way. In this case, the gamer isn't even known—so there is neither censure nor credit for him—but is willing to share his learning publicly.

Post-Mortem Race to the EDGE! Game

WHAT WENT WRONG:

Interface design: In hindsight it would have made things easier and more productive if I had worked more closely with a designer earlier on in the development process.

Planning: I consistently underestimated the amount of development effort required to finish the game.

TAKEAWAYS?

1. I need to learn proper effort estimation.

2. Involve a UI designer in all aspects of the project. Games are a visual medium and need a visually intuitive representation.

3. Developing and publishing a game is a difficult and time-consuming process . . . Though emotionally rewarding, it is financially risky. The business aspect of development and publishing needs to be taken as seriously as the technical aspects.

Finally, cookie baker Gloria Mercer, whom you've seen elsewhere in this book, shared a bit of how she made a mistake and how she learned to improve based on feedback she received. Some spinoff learning during her cookie-training phase was the need to develop photography skills. The next column shows what she posted on her Facebook business page.

Showing mistakes offers enormous insight into how work gets accomplished, and how to improve on it. Culture matters here: Do you want mistakes hidden away, likely to be repeated later, or surfaced so they can be kept from happening again?

 Much Ado about cookies
My sweet sister suggested that I take my eagle cookie picture on a dark background. I think she is correct. So much better. Who would have known that when I said, "I want to know how they make those beautiful cookies." I would be also trying to teach myself how to do photography. This is a learning adventure, if you see how I can learn, tell me. That's what friends are for.

Unlike · Comment · Share · 👍8 💬4 📝1 · 35 minutes ago · 🌐

PRESERVING INSTITUTIONAL KNOWLEDGE

One of the tragic flaws of email is that not only is conversation locked inside a back-and-forth between two people, when in many cases it would be better shared "out loud," but also that when one of the principals retires or leaves, the account is deleted. Whatever might have been there of value would have been difficult to extract, and now it's gone forever. The person who leaves behind work narrated via a blog or through shared presentations, or via images captured during a tricky repair and posted to the work unit wiki, is helping to preserve institutional knowledge for those coming after.

IMPROVING PUBLIC PERCEPTION AND AWARENESS OF WORK AND EFFORT

An organization successful at showing its work offers not just "What we can sell you" information but presents interesting accounts of work that that shows "what we *do*." This can be especially useful for non-profit endeavors, those staffed with volunteers, and those supported by donations or tax dollars, as it says,"*This is what we do with that money*." https://www.facebook.com/pages/Toronto-Wildlife-Centre/155768073655?ref=ts&fref=ts

The Toronto Wildlife Centre narrates its work, and generates a great deal of community engagement, via frequent Facebook updates. In April 2013 a post requesting donations for an injured coyote resulted in a huge community response and subsequent requests from the public for updates on the coyote's condition. Since then, many people have been posting on Toronto Wildlife Centre's page asking for updates on the coyote. Generating such a specific level of interest is an enormous boon in connecting with the public.

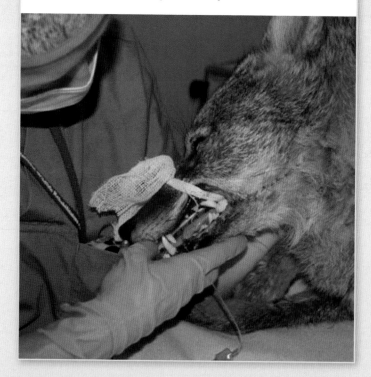

Toronto Wildlife Centre
April 22

UPDATE: The snared coyote had his third surgical procedure today, to suture the area that had opened up and become infected on Friday. His infection is clearing up very well and the skin and flesh around his mouth is starting to look healthier. In this photo, we can see the extent of his wounds on either side of his face from the snare, now stitched up. He is continuing on painkillers, antibiotics, and lots of rest.

BETTER CUSTOMER SERVICE

Showing work can also result in enhanced service to customers. Christopher Groskopf says of the "mountain" of open source code he and colleagues developed during his time on the *Chicago Tribune*'s News Applications team: "More important than any individual project, we've found ourselves in the midst of an exploding community of news-oriented developers who are hell bent on using, contributing to, and releasing new open source code . . . This works for our industry because, with very few exceptions, none of us are in competition with one another. We can share code with the *Washington Post*, *ProPublica*, or the *New York Times* at absolutely no cost to ourselves. This collaboration allows all of us to serve our readers better."

http://blog.apps.chicagotribune.com/2011/09/02/show-your-work/

REDUCING SPACE BETWEEN LEADERS AND OTHERS

Richard Edelman, CEO of the world's largest independent PR agency Edelman PR, regularly posts to his first-person "6 AM" blog. Some posts are about business in general; others share insights gained via a personal experience; still others offer a frank revelation about decision making or activities that affect his organization and its workers. For example, a January 7, 2013, post titled "Paid Media—A Change of Heart" describes his reasoning for changing a long-held position. The blog—which invites comment—builds trust, supports an atmosphere of openness, reduces pushback and outcry, and helps everyone understand how the leader thinks. (See http://www.edelman.com/p/6-a-m/paid-media-a-change-of-heart/ for the post)

OTHER BENEFITS OF SHOWING WORK

↪ Supports recruitment. Showing work via public channels communicates "real" information about the company, the people, the work, and the ways in which workers spend their days.

↪ Disaster prevention/continue the flow. Narrating work answers questions such as:

What happens if _____ resigns or retires?
What happens if _____ is out sick?
What happens if I transfer?
What happens if I am out sick?

↪ Connecting with remote or scattered staff

Lowe's Companies believes in working out loud. In describing the Lowe's "Open Leadership" initiative, Sandy Carter reports that the workers who offered the best tips turned out to be those located farthest from headquarters.

http://www.socialfish.org/2012/11/how-do-you-work-out-loud.html

↪ Enhances employee morale

"One of the main intrinsic motivators is for people to see a purpose in their work. Visibility allows us to make connections to our coworkers, companies, and society at large."

~ Tullis & Crumpler, http://nextthingsnext.blogspot.com/2011/04/whats-vis.html

↪ Supports informal, social, and peer learning

↪ Supports the popular organizational talk about "collaboration"

ORGANIZATIONAL COMMUNICATION CASE STUDY: NASA'S MONDAY NOTES

Here is an overview from Dr. Roger Lanius of a very effective organizational communications system.

[A novel management approach] was pioneered at the Marshall Space Flight Center (MSFC) by its director, Wernher von Braun. This was the "Monday Notes," a management tool he developed during the early 1960s.

Originated as a means of enhancing communication among managers, it was especially intended to deal with the communication gap while Kurt Debus, working much of the time in 1960-1962 at Cape Canaveral, Florida, was away from Huntsville, Alabama, where the Marshall Center was located. Simplicity was the key: no form was required, one-page maximum length, only header was the date and the name of the contributor.

Von Braun asked each of his senior managers to send him once a week a one-page, paragraph-style description of each week's progress and problems. Submitted each Monday morning, it dealt with the previous week's events and von Braun encouraged his reportees to offer totally candid assessments, with no repercussions for unsolved problems, poor decisions, and the like. This Monday Note became so successful as an informal communication tool that von Braun asked about two dozen other officials at MSFC to also send them in. Soon, those sending in notes were not just immediate subordinates, but also lab directors, project managers, and other selected key personnel. In many instances they were two of three levels below the Marshall Center director.

Von Braun read each note and wrote margin comments congratulating success, asking questions, making suggestions, or in some instances giving more negative feedback. After the review by von Braun, his secretary duplicated the entire package of Monday Notes and marginalia, and sent a set to each of those who submitted them.

These Monday Notes made possible important communication between leaders at MSFC. These became another tool—in addition to briefings, informal meetings, and memoranda—for the center director to keep informed of problems and progress. These provided easy and direct access to the MSFC director for managers two or more levels below; no middle-management edited the notes before they went forward. They also prompted the senior leadership at MSFC to pause once a week and reflect on what had been accomplished and to consider the problems to be resolved.

Everyone who has discussed the role of the Monday Notes at Marshall have concluded that the feedback function from the MSFC director was critical to their success as a management tool. It made possible a greater degree of vertical communication at the center, but it also facilitated horizontal communication between organizations, because each person sending a note got copies of everybody else's, thereby learning what other organizations were doing.

Every week managers at MSFC stopped to read what their peers had communicated to von Braun and how he had responded. It served as a court of last resort in resolving differences between organizations at MSFC. The notes also sometime acted as legal briefs presented to an arbiter. Subordinates used the notes as a tool to place before von Braun their perspectives on difficult issues and to advocate their particular solutions. They knew they could get the attention of senior management and a resolution to a problem when raised in this manner.

The requirement to send a Monday Note also prompted many of the subordinate managers to improve internal communication in their organizations. Many required their subordinates to work up similar short notes for them, from which they prepared their inputs to von Braun. It forced virtually everyone in a leadership capacity at MSFC to pause once a week to reflect on what had been accomplished and to consider the problems to be resolved.

The Monday Notes illustrated two general principles in management:

⊖ Made healthy *conflict* between organizations and persons at MSFC a realistic and useful management tool. The freedom (as well as the forum) to disagree was critical to the success of the organization. Disagreements that surfaced in the Monday Notes ensured that a variety of options and solutions were advocated. Evidence indicates that von Braun encouraged this type of conflict and was delighted that the notes were used to express it.

- The notes built *redundancy* into the management and communication system at MSFC. They ensured that all sides were heard. They created additional channels of communication both up and down the organization and across offices at MSFC.

Over time these notes became too bureaucratic—they were at one point institutionalized with forms—they ceased to be useful management tools. At that point they tended to be thought of as just one more report to file, and the time taken in doing it was time wasted in the accomplishment of the mission. Immediately, the quality of the notes fell, and they ceased to provide as much information to the MSFC leadership. Moreover, after von Braun left as director in 1971 his successor stopped making comments on the notes; they ceased to be useful for top to bottom communication.

- This communication system seemed to work best when it was a relatively informal, free-wheeling method of providing information directly to the center director, and back to all the key official. When it was formalized and institutionalized, the bureaucracy beat the liveliness out of the system. In that setting it became just one more form to be filled out, just one more report to be filed.

- The system also worked well when it had two-way communication direct to the top and direct back to the bottom in the form of marginal comments.

- The notes were also successful when they were freely distributed to all contributors.

- The notes also worked best when they allowed the raising of controversies and explanation of divergent positions on important matters within MSFC.

From: http://launiusr.wordpress.com/2011/02/ 28/comments-on-a-very-effective-communications- system-marshall-space-flight-center%E2%80%99s-monday-notes/

Here is an example of a Monday Note. The handwriting at the top is von Braun's and the "B" denotes his review.

The Monday Notes are public record. They are archived and available for viewing at http://history.msfc.nasa.gov/vonbraun/vb_weekly_notes. html.

NOTES 10-26-64   CLINE   B 11/28

1. LH2 EXPERIMENT, SATURN IB SA-203, 204: Participation of Douglas Aircraft Company personnel was initiated immediately. Douglas Aircraft Company will receive authorization for the initiation of engineering design, procurement of long lead-time items, and installation of bracketry in the tank. This is presently in process. To meet the SA-203 launch schedule, installation of one 30-foot dish at each of the four tracking stations would have to be accomplished about 3-6 months earlier than the present installation schedule. This might become a problem. Negotiations with NASA Headquarters are under way. The expected completion date for this effort will be available within one week.

2. BOMB TESTS ON 200K H-1 ENGINE UTILIZING TYPE 5582 INJECTOR END IN ROUGH COMBUSTION CUTOFF: Three tests on two samples of the Type 5582 injector (selected for Phase III of Improved Isp Testing) ended in rough combustion cutoff during bombing at thrust levels about 215K. A parallel effort has been initiated on the Type 5682 injector, which has approximately the same performance as the 5582 and has damped successfully after bombing at thrust levels up at 221K.

Eberhard Please look into this. B

3. MECHANICAL SUPPORT EQUIPMENT MISSION CONTRACTS: When the decision was made that this Laboratory should utilize The Boeing Company (Saturn V) and Chrysler Corporation (Saturn IB) for mission contractors, 11-1-64 was contract award target date. This date was later placed at 12-1-65, and now it appears that this date will slip, particularly in the Saturn IB area. Some action must be taken to speed these contracts toward finalization. To continue to work under task assignments is cumbersome so far as turning over the mission responsibility to each respective party.

I hope this is a printing error! B

BENEFITS TO ORGANIZATIONS?

Showing work offers increased efficiencies, the possibility of innovation and increased ability to improvise, and promises correction of longstanding deficits in organizational communication. Organizations seeking to leverage the potential will find themselves more flexible and agile, and will be better positioned to respond to exceptions, turnover, and sudden changes.

Write something: "The published word is a declaration of membership in that community and also of a willingness to contribute something meaningful to it." Writing creates a deliberateness and encourages reflection.

GAWANDE, *BETTER*

Saying, "I don't have time to narrate my work" is akin to saying, "I'm too busy cutting down the tree to stop and sharpen the saw."

Workers:
What's In It For You?

As we'll see in the "why people share" section, benefits may be as simple as wanting to show off a bit, wanting to pay a community back, or seeking feedback from peers in your field. Whether work gets shown or not, and how well, ultimately rests with the individual worker. Finding easy ways of getting it into the workflow—through quick videos, images instead of paragraphs on weekly reports, or a voice blog post from a mobile phone—may make all the difference.

Saying, "I don't have time to narrate my work" is akin to saying, "I'm too busy cutting down the tree to stop and sharpen the saw." ("I'm a busy knowledge worker. I don't have time to think.") You're already talking about your work, probably more than you know. How can you make that more available to others?

A challenge is the reality of perceived productivity: clients pay us to produce, not reflect; organizations want activity, not journaling. But learning how and what (and when) to narrate work will, in the long run, help to streamline processes, help you develop an awareness of your own best practices, help you see where you are making mistakes, using flawed thinking, and spinning your wheels—and ultimately help improve your final work products and output. It won't hurt if you ever decide to look for new employment, either. So what are some benefits individuals might find through showing their work?

ESTABLISHING CREDIBILITY/EXPERTISE

37signals designer Mig Reyes shares the importance of choosing the appropriate typeface to support your message. Who would you listen to if you wanted an expert on understanding how font affects design, and impact?

Designing Outward

"Blog" has such a temporary, read-and-forget tone to it. On SvN, we take our time writing and editing every article. So rather than treating this like a "blog," I shifted the mindset to that of a tenured publication. So, the entire redesign process started with typesetting the post, and designing outward.

Instead of poring over other blogs, I spent a week studying books, magazines, and of course, Bringhurst. Capturing the right feel for body text was step one—it sets the tone from here on out.

Perhaps it's me, but there's something about `13px sans-serif` faces on the web that feels like "my Rails app just spit this out of a database." I want you to read articles, not text rendered on a screen. Kepler, set at a comfortable size, wound up being a beautiful serif that added the touch of humanity I was looking for. Setting the headlines in Acta added to the look I was going for, and Freight Sans wound up being a great sans-serif pairing.

http://37signals.com/svn/posts/3285-the-typography-and-layout-behind-the-new-signal-vs-noise-redesign

RAISING YOUR PROFILE

When Craig Taylor moved to a new company, one of the first requests he received was for help from a business unit wanting to improve their presentations. He took an existing slide deck and made changes, but better: he kept the old slides at the end and used the speaker note section to explain problems, what could be improved, and why he made changes. While another L&D unit might have created a 10–minute "good PowerPoint" tutorial, Craig gave back a real solution to a real work problem, in context. It was a good call. The unit was very happy with the final product. That, in turn, generated positive buzz about him, helped make him more visible to others, and established him as a go-to guy for this. It also let his new managers see what he could do.

IMPROVING PERFORMANCE

Working out loud can help build the connections vital to learning not just what is done but how work gets done, and how to get better at it. This happens outside of databases and APIs. SAP's Sameer Patel offers an example he's recently seen: "Networks of nurses looking to train each other not on standard policy stuff but tiny tips and tricks in the operating room that reduce latency and risk. These are contextual and very situational and where the 'what's in it for me' is crystal clear to all participants."

(From http://www.pretzellogic.org/blog/2013/06/09/networked-enterprises-social-business-forum-sbf13/)

CREATING DIALOGUE

Sometimes showing work isn't just about declaring something but asking. On June 27, 2013, the author, looking for ideas about framing this book, asked for help from her Twitter-based #lrnchat colleagues. A 60-minute #lrnchat on "Show Your Work" generated *forty-three pages* of conversation around how, what, benefits of, and barriers to, narrating work.

Tracy Parish @Tracy Parish   27 Jun

@MattGuyan Great start with just finding collaborators. RT Q3 improved communication, collaboration #lrnchat

💬 View conversation   ↩ Reply ⇄ Retweet ★ Favorite ••• More

David Kelly @LnDDave   27 Jun

Q2) Narrating work can make someone aware of gaps and opportunities in work that may not be apparent in subconscious workflows. #lrnchat

💬 View conversation   ↩ Reply ⇄ Retweet ★ Favorite ••• More

GETTING HELP: AUTHOR'S STORY

One afternoon a few years ago I received a phone call: The Governor's office needed a writer to help with a "Code of Conduct" for all employees. For the state government workforce, that means kindergarten teachers and registered nurses and prison guards and kitchen workers and Highway Patrol officers, and everything in between. The Governor's office sent over a draft code, a list of seven items they wanted to include, with a little supporting text. One of the items was "Professionalism." I worked in state government for a long time, and every legislative session brings renewed interest in "performance management." So I've been down the road of defining "professionalism" half a dozen times with very little consensus. It is a nebulous concept and tends to be something very much in the eye of the beholder. I knew coming up with a definition that covered this item would be a challenge.

So I decided to ask my Twitter-based PLN (personal learning network) for help. Before I went to work on the remaining six items, I set up a Google Doc, set it to be editable by anyone who accessed it, and tweeted the above message out:

Jane Bozarth @JaneBozarth

**Help w project for Gov's office? Definition of "professionalism" approp for all state emps? Edit: https://docs.google.com/document/d/11/_KeY Hd3OW Thanks!

💬 View conversation   ↩ Reply   ⟲ Retweet   ★ Favorite   •••More

Here's the Google Doc after a few people had edited it:

professionalism

File   Edit   View   Ins   Last edit was made on April 12, 2012 by anonymous

"Profession" comes from Latin roots meaning to make a public declaration. It's still used that way in the Catholic church for the taking of vows by priests, brothers, and nuns...(the profession of vows = the taking of them)
(Can you tell this is Dave F.? I'll make my comments blue.)
So that has me musing about your publicly affirming / proclaiming yourself through your work. That's some spin on "his work speaks for itself."

The challenge is that "professionalism" is one of those words that everyone figures has the same meaning for everyone else (like "learning objective," "understand," and "fair" [the adjective]). So as with performance improvement, I'd look for what people think the *results* of professionalism are, the indicators from which we infer that someone's been professional in the best sense. yeah, "best sense" is just as contextual as "professional." Sorry.

Hi Dave it's Jane-- this is for wide varied workforce and some really don't get 'results' apart from not letting prisoners escape. I think we can address some of this in other areas--it's only one item on a longer list. "Professionalism" was the one I knew I'd have a hard time with. Thanks, JB

THIS IS JASON: LOOKS GOOD TO ME THANKS FOR LETTING ME HAVE INPUT . Can' t find strike through so put strikes in gold highlight. "Altruism" probably not quite right for your prison guards? jw

Meanwhile, I went on dealing with the rest of the items on the document. When I went back to check on "professionalism" the group had edited it down to a final definition. I copied and pasted it in and sent it verbatim to the Governor's office.

Professionalism

Approaching work in the spirit of collegiality, commitment, and accountability. Putting in an honest day's effort while caring about our work and working toward successful accomplishment of it. Doing things well even under challenging circumstances, and carrying out our work because it is the work we have accepted to do.

Good? Yes. Appropriate for kindergarten teachers, prison guards, and kitchen workers? Yes. Better than I could have done on my own? YES.

Most people who know me wouldn't expect this to be the kind of task that crosses my path, as I am most often involved in workplace learning matters. Saying "this is what I do, this is what I'm working on, and I need some help" will usually get you just that. Even better: It can create something others can use. When I showed this during a webinar, so many people asked for a copy of it that I tweeted it back out again and put it on a Pinterest board. It has also spread geographically: I used this as an example during a "Show Your Work" conference presentation in Chicago on September 20, 2013. The following Monday I received an email from a conference attendee who'd taken the idea home with him to Australia:

Date: Mon, 23 Sep 2013 05:43:03 +0000
From: Lee Woodward <lee.w@realestateacademy.com.au>
Subject: Professionalism
To: "info@bozarthzone.com" <info@bozarthzone.com>

Hi Jane
Saw you speak last week and was inspired to make an in house poster of your words on professionalism.
This will hang in our office, on a wall near the kitchen.
Regards,
Lee

PROFESSIONALISM

APPROACHING WORK IN THE SPIRIT OF
COLLEGIALITY, COMMITMENT & ACCOUNTABILITY

PUTTING IN
AN HONEST DAY'S EFFORT
while caring about our work
AND WORKING HARD IN THE
SUCCESSFUL ACCOMPLISHMENT OF IT.

Doing things well
EVEN UNDER CHALLENGING CIRCUMSTANCES
AND CARRYING OUT OUR WORK
BECAUSE IT IS THE WORK WE HAVE ACCEPTED TO DO.

GETTING HELP: NEW WAYS OF WORKING AND COMMUNICATING AT YAMMER

Yammer's Paul Agustin found that the move to Yammer changed his perception of how work gets done and how effective communication looks: "In my previous jobs the communication has followed a slow and inefficient path, like: Managers delegate work, information went back and forth, and data resided in email or a shared drive with no real collaborative abilities. Yammer uses a new model: it's a completely different way of communicating. For instance, I'm currently working on a project in New York with a colleague in San Francisco. We use real-time collaborative notes. Someone gets @ mentioned (at mentioned) in the conversation to draw them in. Allison in Arizona sees it, chimes in, and suggests someone else."

Another advantage? Time. More from Paul Agustin: "Well, say you're working on a course for developers. I can set up a group specific to that topic and ask for input. People can @ each other to pull the right expertise in. They can provide insight on customer needs and experiences in the field. This way of working is MUCH faster. The old way it would have taken me a YEAR to get all this information. This way it takes days."

People like to be asked for their opinions and ideas; showing your work can be another avenue for creating dialogue and getting feedback. Thinking about how you're asking is a way both of getting help and letting them know what you do. Here's an example from IBM's Luis Suarez.

Google+

Luis Suarez

On September 24th I will be in Zurich speaking at JAC 2012 on the Future of Work. I'm currently debating whether I should be the *traditional me* or the *Hippie 2.0* me or perhaps something in between. I'm feeling a bit rebellious and therefore Hippie 2.0 might be best. Hmmm. Thoughts, please? [Thanks!]

PS current themes & topics I plan to cover: Wirearchy, openness, collaboration, honesty, transparency, collaboration, sharing (knowledge), meritocracy, engagement, etc., etc.

Add to circles

Works at IBM as a Social Computing Evangelist #lawwe

Attended University of Salamanca

Lives in Gran Canaria

View full profile

"Quite often the answers to problems that are plaguing you can be gained by educating someone else about the problems you face . . . during the process, you will see the answers for yourself."

~**WASKO & FARAJ,** 2000, p. 167

AN ASIDE: PUBLIC V PRIVATE?

Is there really a reason the conversation about "professionalism," or Luis's request for help with a presentation, should have been locked inside a firewall? Really? If it saves time and gets you a good result, and has nothing to do with proprietary information or potential profit . . . does is really have to be private? Weigh risks and payoffs: In the "code of conduct" example, is the value of protecting the organization's code of conduct from public viewing so important that the better input from outside wasn't worth seeking? Is there something so proprietary that it can't be shared for reuse? Are there circumstances when it would make sense to have your public or your customers help you develop your code of conduct?

REPLACING RÉSUMÉ WITH SOMETHING MORE MEANINGFUL

A portfolio or other document is more than just a résumé listing skills or even accomplishments: It shows how you think, why/how you make decisions, how you work, and what leads to what results.

It's not just "I can do *this*" but "See? I can do this." The best can show not just final products but why/how you got there. Look at the difference in these two job candidates. In the second sample, a workflow outline from professional sketchnoter Sacha Chua, we see not only a finished product but documentation of how she did it. And she makes this available to the public via a shared Evernote notebook.

What else do you need to know about Sacha Chua? Can you see how she does what she does? Do you have a good view of her final product? Do you really think a résumé would tell you more? *Think about the ensuing job interview: who seems more likely prepared with good answers?*

(By the way: The author was recently involved in a hiring situation with the goal of bringing on an e-learning developer. Half of the candidates did not have portfolios available. Who would you choose to interview—or not?)

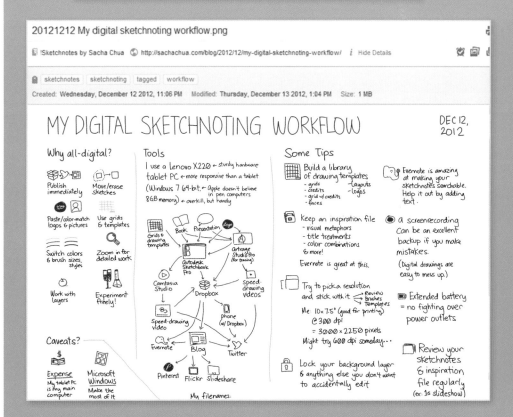

EXPLAINING YOUR THINKING
HELPS YOU LEARN

The report of a Vanderbilt University study published in 2008 discusses an experiment in which young children were shown a series of patterned bugs and asked to guess the next one in the sequence. The children were divided into three groups: one group was asked to simply state the right answer, another to describe their thought process quietly to themselves, and the third to explain their reasoning to their mothers. All three groups were then given another, more advanced pattern test. Researchers found the group that had explained answers to their mothers did better on the more difficult test. Bottom line: When we're asked to articulate ideas to other people, we learn better.

(B. Rittle-Johnson,M.Saylor, K. Swygert. (2008). Learning from explaining: Does it matter if mom is listening? *Journal of Experimental Child Psychology, 100(3)*, pages 215–224.)

TEACHING OTHERS IMPROVES PRACTICE

Teaching others—whether hands-on as with decorating cookies, or through providing a demonstration like one offered by topiary artist Pearl Fryar—forces us to pay more attention to how we do what we do. Rather than just say, "This is what I do," saying, "This is how I do that" brings about reflection and helps us to articulate specific behaviors and detailed steps. In other words: teaching helps you learn.

REFLECTION IMPROVES PRACTICE

Reflective practice is a challenge: we are all busy, and it is human nature to finish one thing and move on to the next, especially when working against deadlines or other pressures. But just taking a moment to say, "What went well? What would I do differently next time?" Can make the next time, and the time after that, go more quickly or smoothly or successfully.

There are a number of disciplines that require, particularly during training, documentation of reflections. Student and entry-level social workers, lawyers, and teachers, for example, are often tasked with journaling or recapping activities and commenting on them. This helps to both capture what happened as well as offer the time and space to develop additional perspectives and alternative explanations or questions. For instance, see what a student nurse wrote.

Show Your Work 5   ♥ Like 7

STUDENT NURSE:

"While I felt very prepared to provide my patients with basic care, I was surprised by my own discomfort at bathing an adult man (instead of the practice manikin). Shifting my learning from textbooks and practice lab settings to human beings may take a bigger jump than I anticipated. I dealt with this in the moment by putting myself in his shoes—being relatively helpless immediately after surgery and having to be so dependent on strangers like me for the most basic care. As uncomfortable as it was for me it was likely more so for him—plus, he was in pain and probably a bit frightened about the whole hospital experience.

I found empathy in a place within myself where I had not looked for it before."

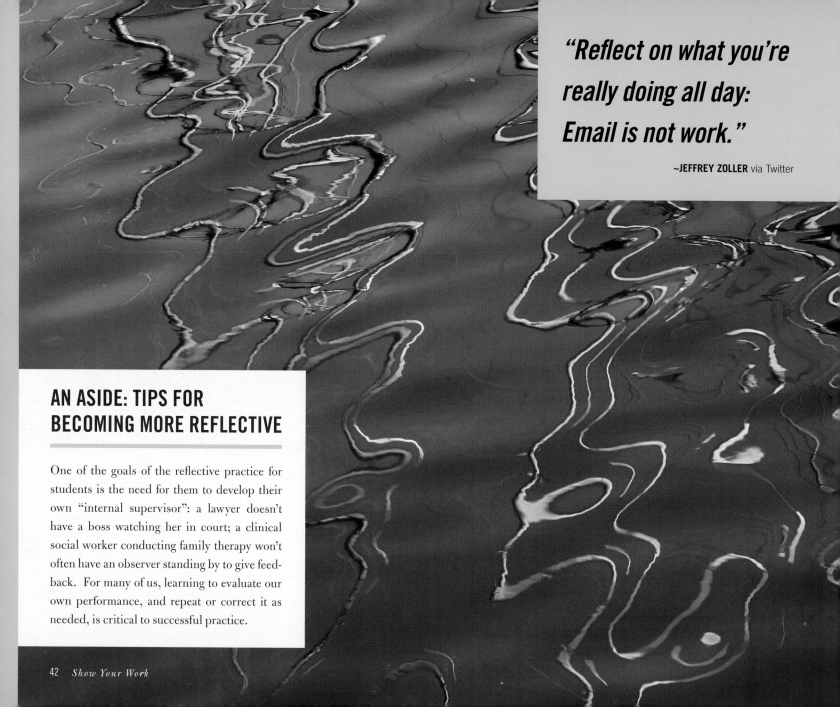

> *"Reflect on what you're really doing all day: Email is not work."*
>
> ~**JEFFREY ZOLLER** via Twitter

AN ASIDE: TIPS FOR BECOMING MORE REFLECTIVE

One of the goals of the reflective practice for students is the need for them to develop their own "internal supervisor": a lawyer doesn't have a boss watching her in court; a clinical social worker conducting family therapy won't often have an observer standing by to give feedback. For many of us, learning to evaluate our own performance, and repeat or correct it as needed, is critical to successful practice.

EXERCISE 1

If reflective practice is new for you, begin by ending a task, particularly a big one, by asking yourself some basic questions. Consider things like:

What do I know now that I didn't know when I started?

Why did this particular (event, barrier, success, accident) happen? How can it be explained?

What can I do differently next time? How could I have made this go (faster, better, more smoothly)?

What political issues emerged ?

A problem I ran into was _____

I fixed it/overcame it/circumvented it by _____

How did the outcome measure up to my expectations?

How well did the actual reflect my estimates on time, challenges, difficulty, people?

I could not fix/overcome/circumvent it because _____

Did this highlight any deficiencies in my preparation/training/skill level? What do I need to do to correct that?

What assumptions did I make? How valid were these? How did they affect what I did?

What do I know about _____ now that I didn't know when I started?

Why did _____ happen? How can it be explained?

What did I learn from this?

EXERCISE 2

Remember the lesson of the patterned bug images and saying it out loud. Linda Kirkman, struggling with managing the content of her thesis, borrowed from ideas on storyboarding and found it most helpful to talk it through out loud, even though the only listener was an admittedly somnolent cat. Her inspiration came from http://patthomson.wordpress.com/2013/03/28/story-boarding-the-thesis-structure/.

Photo courtesy Linda Kirkman (@lindathestar).

Linda says, "The talking really helped me make sense of different ideas. I asked questions such as, 'Why does that go there, why not elsewhere? What is the boundary for that idea? What makes it relevant?' If I had just thought silently about the lacement of the points within the themes it would have taken longer and not been as effective. There is something about speaking the thoughts that clarifies them. I felt less of a dork talking to yourself by imagining the somnolent tortoiseshell cat Charlotte as an audience."

EXERCISE 3

Make yourself a quick printable template and keep a stack handy. Read it over and answer the questions as you complete big tasks, new tasks, or challenging conversations.

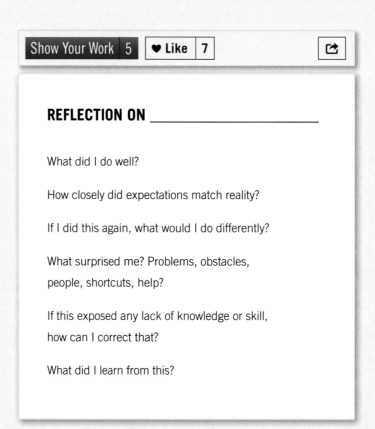

Show Your Work 5   ♥ Like 7

REFLECTION ON _____

What did I do well?

How closely did expectations match reality?

If I did this again, what would I do differently?

What surprised me? Problems, obstacles, people, shortcuts, help?

If this exposed any lack of knowledge or skill, how can I correct that?

What did I learn from this?

While it's tempting to do these exercises and keep them only to yourself, stop and ask, "Who else might benefit from this?" Several examples in this book show the power of talking through mistakes made and ways to avoid them next time. Other practitioners would likely find that more useful than "here is my dazzling thing I did."

For an in-depth look at the value of reflective practice—and writing about it—see Atul Gawande's *Complications,* an excellent first-person account of a new surgeon's experience with learning to learn.

Reflective practice

Reflective practice is "the capacity to reflect on action so as to engage in a process of continuous learning," which, according to the origination of the term, is one of the defining characteristics of professional practice."
Wikipedia

"Writing the blog has inspired me professionally: it has helped make me more disciplined with my working habits and it has undoubtedly made me more creative. It can make you more efficient and even work less! **It can make you a better teacher.** In one year I have undoubtedly learnt more than my last six or seven years in the job combined. It engages you in disciplined deeply self-reflective examination of failure, marginal success and barely perceptible improvement." @huntingenglish

PAYING IT FORWARD

Matt Thompson, editorial product manager at NPR, offers some nice commentary about this on the Poynter.Org blog in a piece called "6 Reasons Journalists Should Show Your Work While Learning":

"It's only right to pay it forward. Whether or not you know it, you've benefited from others who've shown their work. This article you're reading was published by an open-source CMS, using open-source database software. There's a better-than-even chance you're using an open-source browser to read it. As Germuska points out, the Internet was built by people saying, 'Here's what I did. How might it work for you? Make it better.' And certainly, if you've learned to code or you intend to start, you'll have relied quite a bit on the kindness of strangers. What goes around should come around."

http://www.poynter.org/how-tos/digital-strategies/150243/6-reasons-journalists-should-show-your-work-while-learning-creating/. (See this book's section on "Why People Share" for more on this.)

BENEFITS TO YOU

The benefits of showing your work range from career enhancement to paying back (and forward). Note throughout the book the ways in which others are doing this. Few of us are eloquent and prolific Richard Edelmans; some of us may prefer a quick narrated slideshow, a few tweets, or a 6-second Vine video. Some may write narratives while others post by voice. The trick is finding ways to get it into your workflow—making it part of everyday practice without it being another onerous chore. The bulk of this book offers examples that should help provide inspiration as well as ideas for easy means of getting showing your work into your work flow.

Share is the new save.

What Is Knowledge? and Why Do People Share It?

WHAT IS KNOWLEDGE? THREE VIEWS

Organizations or individuals not used to talking about so much "sharing" are often a bit incredulous, or suspicious, of the idea. Some of this stems from ideas one holds about the nature of knowledge. Do you see it as: An object, or bits of discrete data that can be captured and codified, independent of a human actor?

-or-

Something embedded in context, in people and communities, subject to negotiation and interpretation?

The first view, knowledge as discrete bits of data, is historically a common one in organizations and ties closely to ideas around formal knowledge management processes. It's also, not surprisingly, tied to the rise of industrialization and a Taylorized view of work: What people "know" can be captured as bits stored in a spreadsheet or database. It is decontextualized, existing independent of the actor, and the organization's goal is to codify it. This codified, stored knowledge is owned by the organization and new knowledge comes from accessing it. In many instances the organizational cart is driving the horse: there are stores of activity reports and blueprints and process maps removed from any context and free of the landmarks important to following a map.

Those of us who've tried to work with such an item know the reality. It is unreasonable to think a single map or diagram can capture everything that is known about a task: "Trying to divorce practice from work itself leaves us with a challenging view of what gets done, and how, and the intricacies of that. Brown and Duguid (1991) write about this at length, discussing the idea of an organization's "maps," those canonical documentations of processes and procedures and whatever else is considered "knowledge": "As a journey becomes more complex, the map increasingly conceals what is actually needed to make the journey . . . the organization's maps can dramatically distort its view of the routes its members take . . . Although the documentation becomes more prescriptive and ostensibly more simple, in actuality the task becomes more improvisational and more complex."

"Need-to-know only preserves the status quo."

~@LIZGUTHRIDGE

The view that knowledge resides in people supports the emergence and support of "experts" within an organization or field. What is known is known in the heads of these individuals. Organizations must identify who they are, with the result of both potential information overload and heavy demands upon the individuals. The irony: the expert whose expertise is in heavy demand may be too busy being an expert to develop new knowledge or increase expertise; experts are eventually reduced to disseminator rather than creator. Where knowledge-as-data is warehoused in repositories, knowledge-as-expertise is often caught in email, employee profiles, and company directories. A couple of other problems: systems may inadvertently exclude people who have not been identified as experts, and, sadly, in some organizations employees hoard their knowledge because they feel it's the only thing they own.

In both these cases whether and what people share is often tied to self-interests and organizational punishments and rewards, including status. Not surprisingly, working in either environment may encourage people to hoard what they know, or for managers to communicate information to employees strictly on a "need-to-know" basis.

The flaw in these views, if one is married to them too tightly, is the very nature of knowing. People aren't very good at telling what they do, and often know more than they can articulate. As noted by Wasko and Faraj (2000), "This tacit component of knowledge has a personal quality which makes it hard to formalize and communicate, and is deeply rooted in action, commitment, and involvement in a specific context." In other words, asking people to write down what they know tends to not get very good answers.

The last view of knowledge holds that it is embedded in communities and exists within habits and routines and shared language and stories. It develops in the context of shared work and interests and collaborative work toward solving a problem. It emerges in conversation, at the water cooler, in communities of practice and discussion forums and chat rooms. Brown and Duguid (1990) describe this as social capital residing "in the fabric of relationships between individuals and individuals' connections with their communities." In this view, unlike the others, the community generates, maintains, and exchanges knowledge and recognizes that it's an intangible resource (not bits in a spreadsheet) that can't be used up. Unlike the "expert," individuals in the community are seen as knowledge resources rather than risk becoming disseminators.

> ## "Knowledge detached from practice distorts and obscures the intricacies of that practice."

~**BROWN & DUGUID,** 1990

BUT WHY WOULD PEOPLE SHARE WHAT THEY KNOW?

"In today's environment, hoarding knowledge ultimately erodes your power. If you know something very important, the way to get power is by actually sharing it."

~ Joseph Badaraggo

A challenge is getting past the "what's in it for me?" mindset. In a culture where knowledge is viewed as an asset, it's only natural to view sharing as tied to some form of reciprocity or reward. Some do approach interactions with a hope of reciprocity, thinking of helping and sharing as a way of "banking" against a future need. But time spent in public conversations on Twitter or LinkedIn or Facebook can tell a lot about people's willingness to share with little expectation of any return. Those who crave recognition and status can find it publicly, whereas they may not inside the organization. Many conversations, though, show a desire to share springing only from "I know this, and I want you to know it, too, because I found it interesting or useful."

OTHER REASONS?

- ⊖ Public good, giving back, paying forward

- ⊖ People want to connect with others

- ⊖ People want to interact with others who appreciate their competence

- ⊖ Having peers view us as knowledgeable and skillful

- ⊖ Interested in maintaining the community or the profession

- ⊖ Recognition that simply having knowledge does not add value. Value comes from participating in conversations, sharing what you know, helping others and getting help.

Sometimes people share information because it was learned the hard way and they realize it might be useful to someone else. David Byrne, in his new book *How Music Works*, reveals startlingly frank information about his financial income related to a particular project. He said, "I thought by being transparent and using my own experience as an example, I could let other musicians see what their options are—and how their decisions might pan out."

As Wasko and Faraj found in their investigation "It Is What One Does: Why People Participate and Help Others in Electronic Communities of Practice," people also share because:

- ⊖ "I get a kick out of feeling competent"

A 1994 study by Constant, Kiesler, and Sproull showed that workers differentiated what they share and why. They viewed things like products (presentations, reports, programs) as assets owned by the company. But what they had learned was shared with colleagues and communities because they found benefit in sharing. In what Constant calls "emotional communion," he says: "Experts will want to contribute to coworkers who need them, who will hear them, who will respect them, and who may even thank them."

- "It's a been there–done that thing: It would have been nice if I'd had this help in the past"

- "It's the right thing to do"

- "How can the world improve, unless we improve it?"

TRUE STORY: "I CARE AND WANT TO HELP"

Yammer staff are known for embracing the idea of working out loud. UK-based Matthew Partovi regularly posts public requests for advice from colleagues and videos workshops he's created, shares them as time-lapse examples of how he works, and offers RSA-style animated recaps ("I'm not so good with writing prose") of conversations with clients. Partovi finds narrating his work builds trust with colleagues and encourages them to share as well, gets him better feedback, shows what he can do, and supports organizational goals of openness and transparency. Sydney-based Steve Hopkins captures narration as storytelling—particularly around how clients are using Yammer—and, like Partovi, shares presentations and rationale and asks for help and feedback. He finds this approach helps him move more quickly and gives everyone's work greater velocity. Really, though, why do they do it? Partovi says, "I care and want to help."

SHARE IS THE NEW SAVE

Given the tools and the emerging interest in sharing we are seeing the beginning of the end of the hand-it-in mentality. Where most readers probably wrote a report and handed it in for a teacher to grade, kids now create presentations and put them on SlideShare, publish them to YouTube, or otherwise make them available to a wider public. It makes no sense when graduates of a leadership academy submit final projects with "organization-wide impact" only to see them graded and placed in a box. Likewise, the view of knowledge in the workplace is changing: everything isn't just stored away in a file cabinet in hopes it can be retrieved later.

AND FINALLY

Showing your work ultimately means everyone won't have to learn everything the hard way.

References

Brown, J.S., & Duguid, P. (1991). Organizational Learning and Communities-of-Practice: Toward a Unified View of Working, Learning, and Innovation. *Organization Science*, 2, 40-57. 1991.

Constant, D., Kiesler, S., Sproull, L. (1994). What's Mine Is Ours, or Is It? A study of attitudes about information sharing. *Information Systems Research*, 5(4), 400-421.

Wasko, M., & Faraj, S. (2000). It Is What One Does: Why People Participate and Help Others in Electronic Communities of Practice. *The Journal of Strategic Information Systems, 9* (2), 155-173.

If what you're doing isn't worth sharing, then why are you doing it?

"This Is How I Do That."

TOPIARIES

While it isn't exactly "teaching," per se, showing your work can go a long way toward helping others learn.

Pearl Fryar, one of South Carolina's treasures, owns a gorgeous topiary garden he makes free to the public. He's a popular speaker and frequently provides demonstrations of his work to community organizations. Taking up a pair of electric clippers, he goes to work on a plant, just talking through what he's doing as he goes: "This is how I do that." Likewise, there are thousands of YouTube videos on everything from "Here's How I Built That Deck" to "How I Use PowerPoint to Create Custom Art" to "How I play 'Stairway to Heaven' on a Guitar." This can be enormously helpful to the practitioner trying to learn, especially one who's a bit past the basics and just wants to see someone else's practice. Want to know more about Pearl Fryar and his work? He's the subject of the indie film documentary *A Man Named Pearl*.

DOCTORS IN SURGERY
WEARING GOOGLE GLASS

Lucien Engelen of ReShape Glass describes initial experiments in having surgeons wear Google Glass while performing operations. Rather than duplicate existing medical video technologies, he found that Glass (which can be broadcast live as well as be recorded for later viewing) gave observers a better first-person view of the work. Unlike technology that allowed for fixed-camera or over-the-shoulder views, Google Glass allows students to look through the surgeon's eyes.

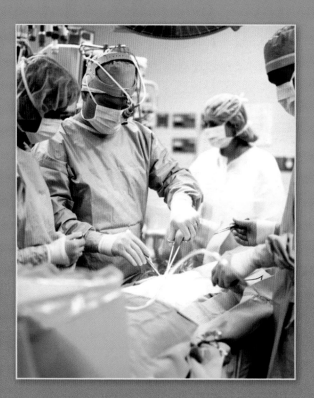

DETAILED BRANCHING
E-LEARNING SCENARIO

Graphic artist and instructional designer Kevin Thorn's award-winning online course "Mission: Turfgrass" takes the learner on a journey more sophisticated than the usual read-click-read-click.

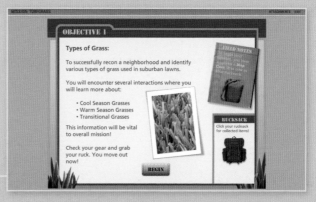

As learners complete the "mission" objectives they accumulate items in a rucksack.

Building this requires careful hyperlinking between the slides (learner achieves objective 1, item goes into rucksack, learner begins objective 2… learner skips to objective 4…). To illustrate how this was built, Thorn offers this schematic.

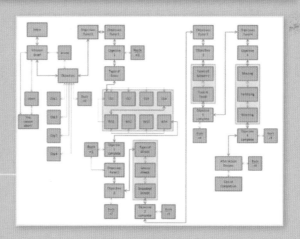

COOKIES BECOME A BUSINESS

Here's a true story of the payoffs of showing work, adapted from an article that first appeared in *Learning Solutions Magazine*. Gloria Mercer, a retired elementary school art teacher, needed surgery on her dominant hand in October 2011 and was told she'd have to find a way to rebuild her strength and dexterity. Thinking, "You should mix something fun with something you need to do, right?" she decided to teach herself to create elaborately decorated bakery-style cookies. Gloria started with YouTube videos, many provided by bloggers whose work she then followed. A lot of her learning was through practice and trial-and-error. And along the way she decided to

share her project with her Facebook friends, mostly because she investing so much time in it and was learning so much from others who were showing their work. Many of her photos included comments about what she was learning, and how.

As Gloria became familiar with the videos and blogs, she developed a growing awareness of an existing active community of people with similar interests. She began engaging with some of the bloggers, asking questions and sharing her own answers. Gloria's daughter Marlo and Gloria's friend Whitney, seeing Gloria's creations on Facebook, decided they wanted to learn, too. Soon *they* started sharing what they were learning; all were participating with the explicit mutual goal of getting better at their new craft (per Etienne Wenger, this is

the very definition of a *community of practice*). As they worked they emerged as contributing members of a true community of practice, with production of artifacts (recipes, actual cookies, and pictures of them), a repertoire (libraries of cutters and techniques mastered, like cartoon characters and airbrushing, and a specialized vocabulary with meaning mostly for other cookie bakers). As they went along, their friends watched, encouraged, suggested cookie ideas, and commented. Eventually, Gloria began teaching others.

Now? Gloria continues to work on her technique, but cookies remain for her only a hobby. Marlo started and operates Coastline Cookies in Midlothian, VA, USA. Whitney started and operates Beach House Cookies in Virginia Beach, VA, USA.

Making Trash

By Gloria Mercer (Albums) · Updated about 6 months ago

So I didn't like the buttercream icing on my cookies because of the texture. I placed them in a bag and told Bill he could eat them. He says, "So. I get to eat the trash." I couldn't stop laughing because he was right.

Unlike · Share

 You, Teresa Greenwood, Trisha Palombo Hamilton, Jamie Mercer Baker and 5 others like this.

 Gloria Mercer It is fun doing what you want to do when you are retired. The lesson I learned from doing 50 cookies is that I would "no" like to do this every week. 50 different cookies for my own fun and learning- Yes!
February 5 at 11:10am · Like · 2

Gloria Mercer "not" is the word. No works too!
February 5 at 11:15am · Like

January 13

January 18. Gloria says she still can't make her hand and icing "do what she wants." Gloria's daughter Marlo, 125 miles away, joins in, as does Gloria's friend Whitney. Gloria describes the need to "stop and stand back" when learning to decorate.

February 2012: Marlo and her husband Mike begin taking orders for cookies. Marlo obtains a business license and Coastline Cookies is born.

April 2012

This weeks cookie time!
By Gloria Mercer (Albums) · Updated about 6 months ago · Taken in Chesapeake, Virginia

This weeks cookies made for my family!

Getting Ready
By Gloria Mercer (Albums) · January 18 · ⏱ · Taken in Chesapeake, Virginia

Getting ready for Valentine's Day. I still can't make my hand and/or icing to do what I want. Takes practice to make pretty cookies.

Cookies are on the way to California
By Gloria Mercer (Albums) · Updated about 3 months ago

May 2012: Spinoff learning: Marlo learns web design so she can launch and manage the Coastline Cookies site.

http://www.coastlinecookies.com/

August 2012: Spinoff learning: Gloria moves on to learning about heat guns, quilting, and cookie photography.

There are so many lessons to be gleaned from this case: the social aspect of publishing your learning, getting feedback and encouragement from friends, and helping other friends as they learn; the fact that enthusiasm can be contagious; the willingness to share and not keep everything to yourself; the real ways that knowledge is "owned" and shared; the organic ways that networks grow.

And more to be learned here: that learning often spawns the desire for additional learning (like web design and photography); the futility of believing we can "capture" knowledge as discrete pieces of data in a spreadsheet; that "generations" has nothing to do with anything; the ways in which social technologies can accelerate learning and give it geographic reach; and the value of a community truly committed to improving practice.

This is social learning. *This* is informal learning. *This* is narrating our work.

Teaching how to make cookies
By Gloria Mercer (Albums) · Updated about 2 weeks ago

Asaf wants to learn cooking making 101

Gloria Mercer
Leaning to use heat gun to dry icing — quilted cookies (4 photos)

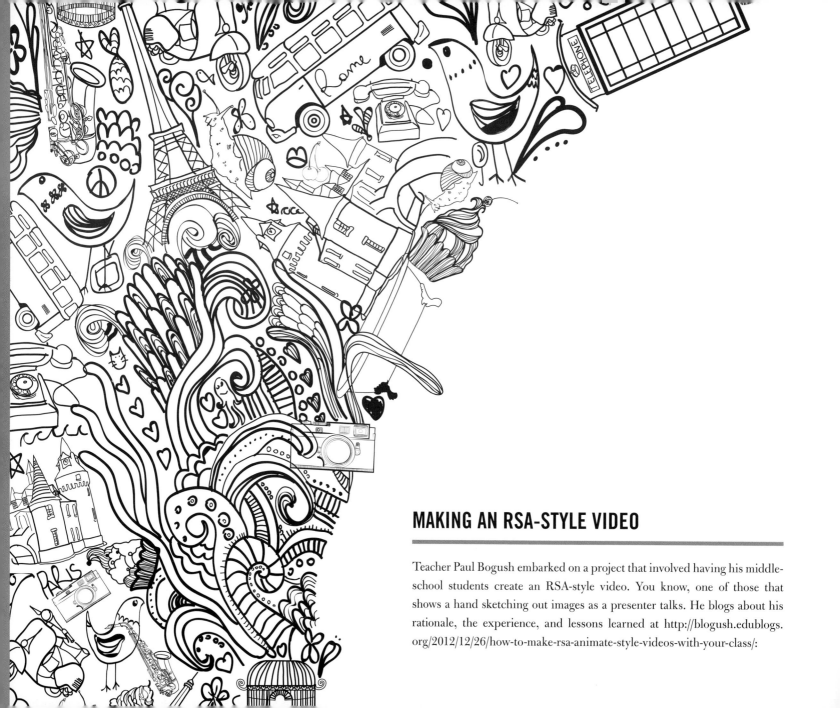

MAKING AN RSA-STYLE VIDEO

Teacher Paul Bogush embarked on a project that involved having his middle-school students create an RSA-style video. You know, one of those that shows a hand sketching out images as a presenter talks. He blogs about his rationale, the experience, and lessons learned at http://blogush.edublogs.org/2012/12/26/how-to-make-rsa-animate-style-videos-with-your-class/:

"This is a unit that was built from the beginning to end with an RSA Animate style video. Please be careful about just slapping any technology onto a unit to make it better. If the unit does not need it, then it is probably best to leave it out. What we have in education is the Instagramafication of teachers' units. Just like people think that they can take a poorly composed picture and spiff it up with Instagram filters and it will suddenly become breathtaking, the same thing is happening in classrooms. Don't just slap on a piece of technology, or in this case an RSA style video at the end just because you can. It won't magically make your unit breathtakingly awesome. You really have to start off by asking why? Why is this tool or method necessary for the success of this unit?

So let's start there…

2012 was coming to a close and I still noticed some important things that my kids could not do yet. They had a lot of trouble making connections between things that they read, not only across multiple sources, but even in a single one. They were seeing each paragraph, each sentence as individual disconnected facts. My guess is that maybe this came from years of "read the chapter, answer the question, spit the question back" without having to put the facts

together into a story and make connections between them. It sounds silly, but yes, what you are reading in the third paragraph happened because of what happened in the first paragraph.

The other problem was that the words they were reading were just that…words. If they read Benjamin Franklin traveled to France, in their heads he just magically appeared there. If they read George Washington crossed the Delaware River, they never pictured a boat…or even water. They are used to simply just reading words and playing a matching game with the questions they received for classwork or homework. One student during this project actually told me that he was having trouble because in the past he would just write down everything from the paragraph and some of it had to answer the question. They also still struggle with reading something long, and making it short…getting right to the point. Another struggle is supporting their point with information from the text they read, and then putting the whole darn thing back into a story.

As I thought about these problems, I decided that making RSA Animate style videos would address all of these. It was an easy way to make them visualize their information, make connections, and re-tell their facts in a story that had a very tight story line that flowed. All skills that would transfer nicely to any traditional essay. I decided on a very straightforward topic, the Louisiana Purchase, and examined it in a very straightforward way without going into some of the nuances of the deal. I also decided to use the textbook as the main source. I have faced the reality that the kids will be reading a social studies textbook and anything I could do to make it less scary allow them to read it more fluently will be a huge help in the next 4-8 years of their life. We also did not have any time for multiple source research, so the text was our default source.

DAY ONE-DIRECTIONS AND READING

On the first day I handed out the directions:

Get to the point...

A great story teller once told me that you should never tell the audience the "point" of your story. Youshould let them figure it out and whatever they interpret as the "point" is correct. She said that is is ok to let an audience walk away with multiple interpretations of a story.

Hogwash...

Sometimes you need to "Get to the Point" and this project is one of those times.

Here is your problem...you need to tell the story of the Louisiana Purchase and at the end of the story it needs to have a crystal clear point. Nobody viewing the story should miss the point. A three year old listening to your story while jumping on a pogo stick should be able to get your point. Get my point? We will do these stories in a style made famous by RSA Animate. We will watch several examples in class.

The set-up:

- Read pages 298-301 in your textbook. Break the story into ten parts, with each part having three pics. Use the staircase method that I will demonstrate in class.

- Write a whu-ha-ha linking each stair (better listen to the in class explanation on that one eh?).

- At the top of the stairs write your one sentence "point" you will make with your story.

- Sketch out each of the pics

- Write the narration for the pics

- As you write the narration, decide which pics will need captions

- As you write the narration, decide which pics will need additional writing to help with a transition from one to another

This is more complicated than it seems. You are telling a story with three mediums: voice, pictures, and written words. Mix them together to suck your audience into your point.

I then showed them some examples of RSA videos. We found a few created by schoolchildren.

At this point it was still hard to figure out how we were going to go from information in a textbook to an RSA Animate style video. I was very honest with them about how I had no idea and we needed to figure out how to do it all together because there was no template out there for us to follow.

The first work they did was to simply read the pages in the textbook on the Louisiana Purchase. I made them put their notebooks and pens away so that they could not take any notes as they read. The idea being that I wanted them to get the whole picture first, instead of picking it apart and writing everything that they read. Next they made ten steps, and placed one point from the story on each step. Each step had to connect to the one prior to it. They were able to have no more than ten, no less than nine. This was not random, I did this beforehand and determined that based on what they read, 10 was the appropriate number. When a kid asked if they could have 14, I knew they were watering something down, and if they asked if they could have 6 I knew they were missing a point in the story. By having ten I actually somewhat dictating what they would write without them knowing it.

Under each step they had to place three facts supporting their step. We talked about how without support the steps

would collapse, and without connecting them a listener would "fall through" and not get the story straight. They had to label each step before writing the supports, and could only support each with three things. Again, based on me doing this I thought that was appropriate. At this point after reading the story, creating the steps, and then evaluating which facts to use for support they had processed the information three times and when listening to them trying to figure out which facts to use could help them making decision based on what happened in prior steps, and what was needed to make the next step make sense.

DAY 2-DRAWINGS

On the second day they tried to figure out how they would visualize each supporting fact. They had to have at least one image per fact. They also had to figure out what types of captions and labels they would need.

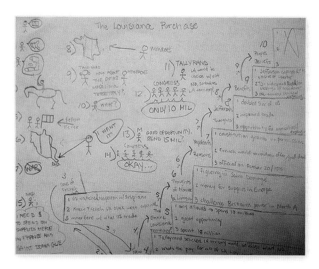

Many kids were concerned about their drawing ability so I told them a story about a bobcat sitting next to three bushes and then drew a very simple picture of a bobcat sitting next to three bushes.

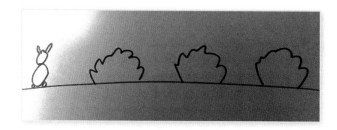

Now what do you see in the image above? A bobcat and bushes right? I then told them a story about a rabbit sitting next to three giant heads of lettuce and drew the same picture. I pointed to the rabbit and asked them "what is this?" The whole class said rabbit. Then I pointed to the "lettuce" and the whole class said lettuce. So I acted a bit confused since it was the same picture and they had just identified the animal as a bobcat…ah-ha moment. People will believe anything you tell them. Everyone became more comfortable. Then I made a big mistake…I told them to make their drawings very simple. They made them too simple and took so little time to draw that when the film speed was increased some drawings were barely visible.

DAY THREE-DRESS REHEARSAL…SORT OF

On day three I made a decision to have them sketch out their entire drawing from start to finish before writing their script.

out on small paper before going large…something I would require next year since it really helped to do a quick version first before going big.

This ended up being a good decision. They really needed to see what their final product was going to look like and this added a jolt of excitement into the project that made them pay more attention to their scripts the next day. It is absolutely necessary that a day gets devoted to practice. After watching, there is no way they could have gone from little pictures next to their steps to doing this for film. Many kids sketched it

When they did a full scale practice some used roll paper and some used whiteboards. I like the idea of having them do it on a large sheet of paper, even though they might eventually do it on a whiteboard. This way they see everything they have drawn and don't forget where they just were, and could look back to help remind them as to where they are going. The same impact could be had on a whiteboard by telling them to not erase anything.

THE PRACTICE DAY WAS SERIOUSLY ORCHESTRATED CHAOS!

When they were done many groups went back and edited images to make them fit and flow better. The kids that did it on paper simply rolled it up so they could use it the next day, kids who did it on whiteboards took pictures with their phones.

DAY FOUR-RECORD THE VIDEOS

The day we recorded the videos was simply wild. Everyone knew that we had just this one day to record, so they could not start over very many times. I would guess that the

average group took about thirty-five minutes to get together, set-up, and record.

The filming went so much better than I anticipated. We really had no idea how to do this so everyone figured it out as we went along. What they learned is that a very tiny camera starts to get very heavy after 20 minutes so they started to set-up in some very creative ways and each class took the best ideas of the previous one.

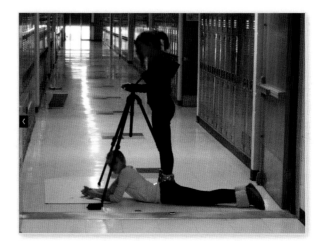

It was important to stress that the kids filming needed to zoom in and focus on what was being drawn. So if a kid was drawing a person, the person should fill the the camera screen. It was also important to stay as still as possible…and I bet you can't guess why. Let's say a kid filming moves ever so slightly while filming, so little that when you watch it you don't even notice it. Now increase the speed of the film 5x…it becomes unwatchable. Luckily what saved us is that on youtube you can click on enhancements, and then stabilize. Without that feature most of the videos would have been unusable.

Some groups did start using tripods-I have two in the class. A huge difference is seen in the final videos that used tripods, but the camera was not able to move as freely…so still undecided what to do next year.

The supplies we needed were actually easier to get than I thought. 3M donated cameras to our school system, but I think between phones and kids bringing in cheap digital cameras we would have been covered. At least a couple kids in each class used their own camera or phone. We used 12 whiteboard markers, which by the end of the day were trashed. Maybe four were still usable. Whiteboard cleaner was a must! We went through two bottles, or at least some kind of cleanser because so much writing was done that in between classes we really needed to totally clean each board. Our wet paper towels stopped working after the first class. Another thing that we figured out is that paper towels and whiteboard erasers simply didn't cut it after a while. We took some sweatshirts that had been in lost and found for months and cut them up. That might have been the best idea of the week.

I had a big roll of white paper that we used that a student teacher left behind ten years ago! The big roll paper used for bulletin boards would have also worked. We used the whiteboard in class, you could fit three groups at once, and I also had a sheet of shower board at home that I cut into four pieces. We also went through a bunch of masking tape. The kids needed it to tape up their practice sheets from the following day so they were easier to follow.

We also established a checklist and place to return everything. You now how it goes…first period accidentally walks off with one marker, second period 2 more markers, by last class you have one marker. So everyone froze before leaving and someone went through the check-list to make sure everything was back where it belonged.

It was important to stress to the kids that they could talk during the filming and give directions and think out loud. The audio in these videos would eventually be muted. Many groups tried to be very quiet out of instinct!

Below is what it would have sounded like if you were in the hallway filming with the kids. You'll see, the above images and videos make the reality much more peaceful!

DAY FIVE-WRITE THE SCRIPTS

I am still going to go with it was a good idea to write the script after the images. Doing the images first allowed them to visualize what they were going to write about, better understand it, and allowed the scripts to flow better and sound more like narration rather than essays. Scripts are absolutely necessary. No one could come up the next day without one. Even the kids who knew the story by heart had to have a script. Simple reasons why…we had enough time the next day to have each group come in and do one take. They would be sitting down and watching their video for the first time, it would be 5-7 times faster than when they originally did it, they would have to be able to on the fly go faster or slower to keep up with the video, and simply no one's brain can do all that processing and keep up. One single ummm would be enough to throw off the entire thing. There was no issue writing the scripts because they essentially just took their supporting details under each step and made them into sentences. While the students were writing the scripts I spent the day processing the videos. We don't have very good computers. The 2gb of RAM is not enough to process a twenty minute video quickly. In my head these were going to be two minute videos, but I forgot that the original file would be around 10-30 minutes long. That is how long it took the kids to film their videos in real time. The videos were shot at 720p, which resulted in a huge huge file. Too big to put into MovieMaker and have the kids watch and narrate at the same time. The file was so large that if we tried to watch it at 5x speed it would freeze. So while they wrote the scripts, I placed each video into MovieMaker, sped it up 5X, and then rendered it into another file.

Each video could take 15++ minutes. I started at 6am and finished at 3:30pm. To give you an idea…using a simple school laptop with 2GB of Ram, each minute of video would take one minute to get loaded into the video editing software, and then to save it as a movie would take almost 2 mins per minute of video. Again…cruddy laptop. Almost every laptop in the world has more than 2 GB of Ram and would do this process faster. One idea next time is to take lower quality video, or do larger groups so there would be fewer videos. If you have better computers, this probably won't be that big of an issue. Also keep in mind that you might need a universal card reader to get the videos off of your camera or cell phones.

DAY SIX-RECORD THE NARRATION

When the kids came in to record the narration they knew that they would have a 5 minute block of time. So they could make a mistake at the beginning, and re-do, but other wise it was probably a one shot deal. So is our schedule in school and the reality is that I knew that there would be people in our community who would not approve of us doing this and spending multiple days on scripts would not be a good thing. If you have time and support for big projects, I think three days would be a perfect amount of time. One day for practice, and two days to record groups with enough time for multiple takes.

Because we were short on time, and quality computers I had a crazy set-up.

I had two computers hooked up. I would have two videos set-up when the class walked in. One group would be recording using one, then I would switch to the other. While the second group was recording I would save the first movie that was narrated and then load up another video on that computer. It is very important to remember that you need to mute the volume in the original video so that their narration is the only audio. So looking at the picture above, the kids are recording their narration on computer #2, and up on the screen #6

is their video playing at 5X speed. I used a very simple microphone #5 that I threw into the middle of the table. While they are doing this computer #1 is saving the narration from the last group, and then I will load up a video for the next group on #1.

So how to switch between the two computers? I had a microphone #3 and speakers #4 hooked into the computer the girls are recording into, and as soon as they were done I would flip the microphone and speakers to computer #1.

To get the video up on screen I had to take the cable that ran to the projector #1 and simply switch it to the computer being used to record. Since my desktop computer obviously does not have a monitor directly connected to it, after you disconnect #1 from it you would have to reconnect the monitor #3 to where #1 was so that you can see what is happening on the desktop while kids are recording using the laptop. Easier than I made it sound! The recordings went smoothly, some kids came back during lunches to either re-do it, or to do it again because they simply kept making mistakes the first time.

Here is a video of a group recording at lunch so the set-up is a bit different.

We added music just messing around to one and what we found was interesting. I think the music is necessary because the kids simply are not great script writers yet and the music makes it more interesting. It also helps fill in the dead air when they got stuck or had nothing to say. Because they did not see the videos before narrating they had no way of knowing how long each step would be, and I only had time to make each video 5X faster than normal, so if we had time we could have messed with the speed, or even changed the speed throughout the video, but again we had 5 minutes per group. The music also helped block out the background sounds of feet shuffling, sniffles, and doors opening and closing. We just threw a bunch of songs into a folder and just

slapped on into each video. Again if we spent more time I think choosing the right music and matching it to the action would have been awesome.

We have 17 videos finished, and will do the rest after break. They are all "finished," we just have to pop the music into most of them and upload. Here is a playlist with the completed videos.

THINGS I WISH I DID...

- Had more rags available

- More cleaner

- No more than 8 groups per class

- Have the kids be more complex in their drawings, and draw slower. There is no rush while filming the drawing.

- Have kids write key words on board that match key words in script to make it easier to glance up and see where they are

- Fix cameras on tripods, music stands, anything

- Better directions for camera people

- Have each video end with a zoom out so that entire board could be seen

- I didn't have enough time to go over anyone's drawing or

scripts in any detail…which is why you hear almost every kid say things like "Haiti." Modern name, not historically accurate.

- Wish added one more day, we never got to really add just a bit more to the research and writing about the implications of the purchase

- Keep in mind, this was our first time, so I kept it simple, maybe next time each video focuses on one aspect of the Purchase, like the Constitutionality of the purchase

This is an activity for any class, not just social studies. Also, pretty much any obstacle you can think of can be overcome. Even if you paired your kids up and each pair did one step and one did only one video per class.

We also talked at the end about how no professional would have worked under the constraints we did. You can read about how one professional did her film by clicking —> here. My kids did an incredible job considering the time and supplies they had. Imagine if they had a chance to practice their drawings twice! Narrate once, check for sound, and then do it again…I could go on and on. It's just if you can give more time to this than I did please do. I think the final products would be awesome. Remember that what you

read about happened during 45 minute periods, so after the teacher yapped for about ten minutes they had about 35 minutes of work time each period. This was also done with incredibly mixed classes. My kids are super, but we are from average town America. If we could do it, so can you and your kids.

Quick common core connection at the end here…one of the things that could be positive about the common core standards is that they want kids to behave like professionals. Do the things, read the things, create the things that real professional artists, historians, scientists, and authors do. I just also hope that they give us the same amount of time that real professionals spend on their tasks. I can only dream of being in a place where we could have spent a week researching, a week preparing, and a week recording…along with decent equipment.

So if you made it this far, you have got to try this. Come back and leave some advice in the comments. I feel like I need to do this for at least three more years before I have a good handle on it!

"THIS IS WHAT I DO ALL DAY": MÉDICINS SANS FRONTIÈRS / DOCTORS WITHOUT BORDERS

We make assumptions that we know what others do all day: "he's just a pencil pusher," "teachers spend all their time in front of a classroom," "the Project Managers are always in meetings." Finding out what colleagues actually do all day can go a long way toward breaking down silos, finding common ground, understanding another's situation and context—thereby building better ideas for communicating and working together—and locating expertise across the organization or across disciplines.

Here's an example of a "day in the life" from Médicins Sans Frontières (MSF)/Doctors Without Borders: "Follow us today as Canadian Doctor Anne Marie Pegg updates a day in the life of a humanitarian aid worker on International Women's Day." The organization posted on both their Facebook page https://www.facebook.com/msf.english and via Twitter. Here are some Tweets from that day, captured in Storify http://storify.com/MSF_Canada/a-day-in-the-life-of-anne-marie-pegg-msf-doctor-in

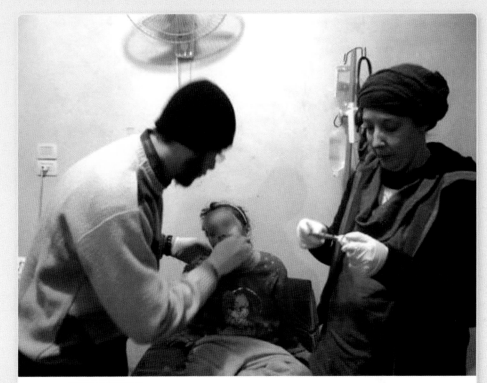

 **MSF CANADA**
@MSF_canada

 Follow

Today Dr AnneMarie Pegg tweets a day in the life of an #MSF aid worker for #IWD2013bit.ly/ZIskwK

9:00 AM - 8 Mar 2013

17 RETWEETS 3 FAVORITES

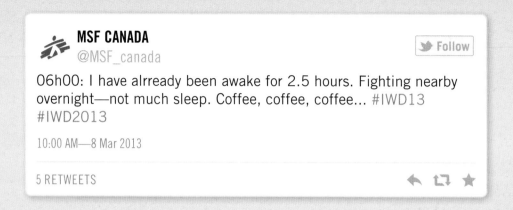

MSF CANADA
@MSF_canada

06h00: I have alrready been awake for 2.5 hours. Fighting nearby overnight—not much sleep. Coffee, coffee, coffee... #IWD13 #IWD2013

10:00 AM—8 Mar 2013

5 RETWEETS

MSF CANADA
@MSF_canada

that (French) sign reads: "Here: The possible is already done. The impossible is underway. For miracles, the wait is 48 hours." ;^)

2:08 PM—8 Mar 2013

1 RETWEET

MSF CANADA
@MSF_canada

00h45: New patient arrival from nearby maternity clinic—labour for hours, no progress. Off to the OT we go for a c-section... #IWD2013 #IWD

3:30 PM—8 Mar 2013

1 RETWEET

Médicins Sans Frontières/Doctors Without Borders (MSF) is an international, independent, medical humanitarian organization that delivers emergency aid to people affected by armed conflict, epidemics, exclusion from healthcare, and natural disasters in more than seventy countries. To learn more visit www.msf.org .

MSF CANADA
@MSF_canada

🐦 Follow

01h30: It's a girl!!! Mom and baby doing well. Not so bad of a reason to still be awake. #IWD2013 #IWD

4:00 PM - 8 Mar 2013

2 RETWEETS 2 FAVORITES

"THIS IS HOW I SPENT THIS DAY": DESIGNING A MOBILE APP

Designer Kevin Thorn was offering a workshop on building a simple performance support reference tool to use on a mobile device. He took photos throughout the day and posted them to a Facebook group of designer friends to show us both the steps in building the actual product and how he taught it. Participants moved from brainstorming ideas, to using index cards to lay out a storyboard of their idea, to wireframing (sketching out how it will look/work to the user), building a prototype, and publishing it online to be accessed on a device. As Kevin was posting photos in real-time, those watching could offer suggestions and ask questions as well.

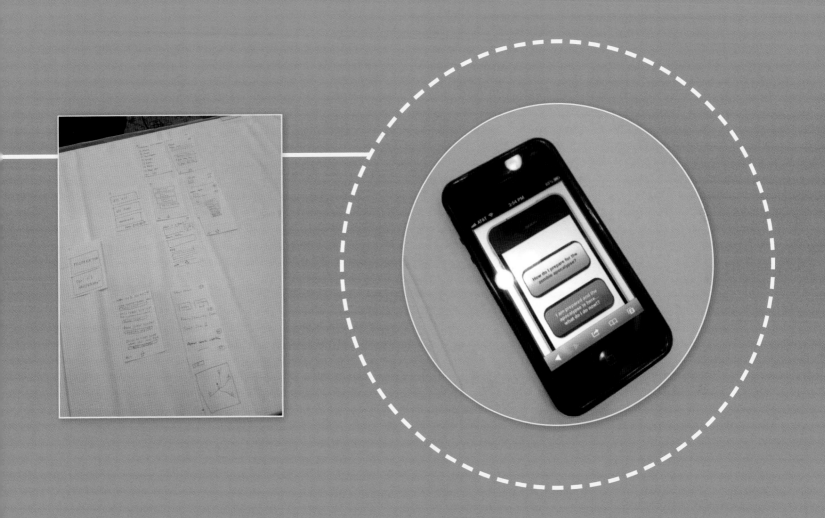

"THIS IS WHAT I DO": THE CONSULTANT

Consultant Steve Woodruff (Clarity Therapist: http://www.stevewoodruff.com/)shares notes from a breakfast meeting at which he helps a client find focus for a job search based on her past roles.

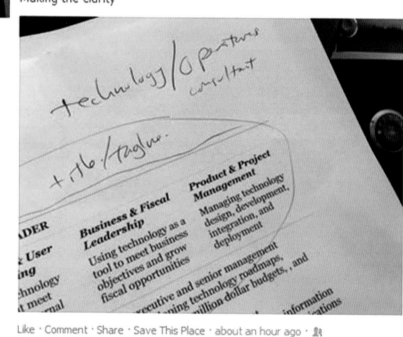

Steve Woodruff
Making the clarity

Like · Comment · Share · Save This Place · about an hour ago · 🐾

Steve Woodruff Helping a friend define his career future, based on a very extensive set of past job roles. Should be a COO and/or high-level business operations architect/consultant IMO.
18 minutes ago · Like

"THIS IS HOW I DECIDED": VISUAL DESIGN CHOICES

Kathy Sierra (aka Seriouspony) reminds us that interviewing experts is often pointless as they really don't know how they made a decision. Finding the few who can, and watching how through reflection and articulation they can share that, might help.

37 Signals designer Mig Reyes talks about the importance of choosing the right font to support your message.

Seriouspony @seriouspony
True experts don't *know* precisely how/what they use to make expert decisions/actions. We interview them & make mistake signal for noise.

💬 View conversation   ↩ Reply ⇄ Retweet ★ Favorite ••• More

Designing Outward

"Blog" has such a temporary, read-and-forget tone to it. On SvN, we take our time writing and editing every article. So rather than treating this like a "blog," I shifted the mindset to that of a tenured publication. So, the entire redesign process started with typesetting the post, and designing outward.

Instead of poring over other blogs, I spent a week studying books, magazines, and of course, Bringhurst. Capturing the right feel for body text was step one—it sets the tone from here on out.

Perhaps it's me, but there's something about 13px sans-serif faces on the web that feels like "my Rails app just spit this out of a database." I want you to read articles, not text rendered on a screen. Kepler, set at a comfortable size, wound up being a beautiful serif that added the touch of humanity I was looking for. Setting the headlines in Acta added to the look I was going for, and Freight Sans wound up being a great sans-serif pairing.

http://37signals.com/svn/posts/3285-the-typography-and-layout-behind-the-new-signal-vs-noise-redesign

"THIS IS HOW I DECIDED": YAMMER

Yammer offers an overview of the product. The video is at https://player.vimeo.com/video/66173844

Allison Michels
@anicole87

Following

Video: Building Yammer for Everyone buff.ly/1bOXcZw << this is why we do things the way we do.

← Reply   ⟲ Retweet   ★ Favorite   ••• More

1
RETWEET

1
FAVORITE

1:58 PM—18 Jun 13

"THIS IS WHAT I DID TODAY": ATTENDING A CONFERENCE

Craig Taylor traveled from England to attend the DevLearn conference in Las Vegas. At the end of each day he offered recaps of the sessions he'd attended, along with key takeaways, to share with colleagues back at home. At the time this screenshot was taken, more than seventy people had viewed it.

http://youtu.be/Lf6VLwxYwRg

"THIS IS WHAT I LEARNED TODAY": ATTENDING A WEBINAR

Heidi Matthews tweeted her takeaway from a webinar session, sharing her notes with the public and with the facilitator.

 Heidi Matthews
@heikan2003

 Following

My notes from today's Bozarthzone webinar. Thanks @JaneBozarth
pic.twitter.com/AbxcVIMWbR

↩ Reply ⇄ Retweet ★ Favorite ••• More

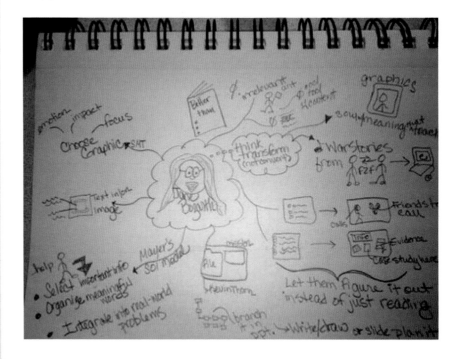

"THIS IS HOW I LEARNED THAT": HOW I TAUGHT MYSELF...

Startup ZenCap's founder David Sinsky regularly blogs about what he's working on. The following blog post gives an overview of a self-directed learning project and ends with a short recruitment pitch.

How I Taught Myself to Code in Eight Weeks

21 Tuesday **Aug 2012**

(originally posted on the Yipit Django blog, later reposted on Lifehacker)

To a lot of non-developers, learning to code seems like an impossibly daunting task. However, thanks to a number of great resources that have recently been put online for free— teaching yourself to code has never been easier. I started learning to code earlier this year and can say from experience that learning enough to build your own prototype is not as hard as it seems. In fact, if you want to have a functioning prototype within two months *without* taking a day off work, it's completely doable.

Below, I've outlined a simple path from knowing nothing about software development to having a working prototype in eight weekends that roughly mirrors the steps I took.

INTRODUCE YOURSELF TO THE WEB STACK
(10 MINUTES)

The presence of unfamiliar terminology makes any subject seem more confusing than it actually is. Yipit founder/CEO Vin Vacanti has a great overview of some of the key terms you'll want to be familiar with in language you'll understand.

GET AN INTRODUCTORY GRASP OF PYTHON AND GENERAL PROGRAMMING TECHNIQUES
(1 WEEKEND)

⊖ **Learn Python the hard way:** Despite the title, the straightforward format makes learning basic concepts really easy and most lessons take less than 10 minutes. However, I found that the format didn't work as well for some of the more advanced topics, so I'd recommend stopping after lesson 42 and moving on.

⊖ **Google's Python class:** Read the notes and / or watch the videos and do all of the associated exercises until you get them right—*without* looking at the answers. Struggling through the exercises I kept getting wrong was the best learning experience. I would have learned far less had I just looked at the answers and tried to convince myself that I understood the concepts.

These two resources are somewhat substitutable and complementary. I recommend doing the first few lessons from both to see which you like better. Once you've finished one, skim through the other looking for concepts you aren't fully comfortable with as a way to get some extra practice.

GET AN INTRODUCTORY UNDERSTANDING OF DJANGO (1 WEEKEND)

↻ Work through the Django tutorial.

↻ Delete all your code.

↻ Work through the tutorial again, from scratch.

The first time I went through the tutorial I inevitably ended up just following the instructions step-by-step without really understanding what each step did since everything felt so new.

The second time through I wasn't as focused on the newness of the concepts was better able to focus on understanding how all the parts work together.

GET A DEEPER UNDERSTANDING OF PYTHON/GENERAL PROGRAMMING CONCEPTS (2-4 WEEKENDS)

↻ **Udacity's intro CS class:** Udacity's courses are generally 7 session classes (2-3 hours per session) that you can at your own pace. (I'm a huge fan of Udacity's pedagogy and recommend the intermediate programming class or the web development class as follow-ups to this two-month curriculum.)

↻ **Unit 1 of MIT's intro CS course:** Really well taught and surprisingly approachable.

Again, I would sample each and see which you like the best. I ended up doing both but that was probably overkill.

PRACTICE BUILDING SIMPLE WEB APPLICATIONS
(1 WEEKEND)

⊝ Work through a few of the exercises in Django by example. These exercises don't hold your hand quite as much as the Django tutorial but they still provide a fair bit of guidance so I found it to be a nice way to start taking the training wheels off.

BUILD YOUR PROTOTYPE
(1 WEEKEND)

⊝ Build a prototype in just one weekend? Yes, you'll be embarrassed by what it looks like (I sure was) but that's the whole point.

That's it. Eight weekends (or less) and you've gone from zero to a functioning prototype. Not so daunting after all is it?

Author's Note: It goes without saying that there's a huge difference between the relatively cursory amount of knowledge needed to build a simple prototype (the focus of this post) and the depth of knowledge and experience needed to be a truly qualified software engineer. If you want to learn all that it takes to build modern web applications at scale, getting professional web development experience at a fast-growing startup like Yipit is a great next step. If you're smart, hard-working, and passionate about creating amazing consumer web experiences drop us a line at jobs@yipit.com—we're always looking for great people to join our team.

http://dsinsky.wordpress.com/2012/08/21/how-i-taught-myself-to-code-in-eight-weeks/

"THIS IS WHY I LEARNED THAT": NEW EMPLOYEE ONBOARDING

New Hires at Aspen Dental are required to post to the class blog, explaining not just what they are doing but what they are learning and how that learning fits into the bigger organizational picture. This can be enormously helpful to the new hire who doesn't always understand why a process or practice exists, or the importance of following it.

Used with permission from Aspen Dental Management, Inc.

AspenDental®

plan of attack

Hi everyone. Today I am hitting the charts! Charting w the dr, entering treatment plans, and sitting in on the consults. The new patient from start to finish! Took a look at the offices' patient-with-credit-balance and it is being worked as we speak.

There were notes and the office manager could describe to me about half of the report where we were with the patients. So I believe It's a benefit to the patients b/c it keeps them a priority to us. We see so many a day, this is a great way to keep any of them from slipping through the cracks.

Posted at 11:27 AM by   Permalink Email this Post Comments (2)

"THIS IS HOW I LEARNED THAT": USING NEW WEB TOOLS

Terry Brock learned to publish to blog from iPad by creating a video talking about how he … published to blog from iPad. From http://terrybrock.com.

"THIS IS HOW A GOVERNMENT AGENCY SHOWS ITS WORK": THE UK MINISTRY OF JUSTICE DIGITAL SERVICES BLOG

In an age when government seeks to be more transparent to its taxpaying public, the UK Ministry of Justice's Digital Services offers a refreshing, frequently updated blog featuring real people enacting real work, free of bureau-cratese and the usual obfuscation. The blog includes the services' live Twitter feed offering shorter, more frequent updates. It is very explicit: "This is what this government agency does. This is who does it. This is what it involves. This is what is accomplishes. This is where your money is going."

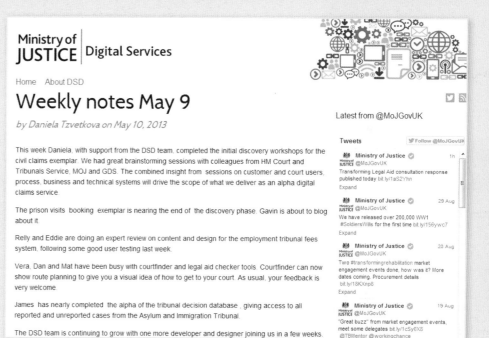

http://blogs.justice.gov.uk/digital/2013/05/weekly-notes-may-9/

"THIS IS HOW I CREATED THAT": MATT GUYAN

"Showing My Work"

Recently at my workplace, I've been involved in a project to train a group of employees to become relief operators for some items of plant (which are machines like tractors, graders, excavators and trucks). I was working on this project with the HR Co-ordinator and the L&D Officer for the outdoor staff in our organisation. My role as the instructional designer was to develop some materials to help the new operators learn how to drive and use the various machines (there were 9 different types in all).

Armed with a Sony Handycam, we met with each operator who was also our subject matter expert (SME). The reason for filming was that we thought it would be easier to capture what the SME was saying and showing, rather than having to make lots of notes and take photos. The SME took us through the pre-start checks, what the cabin controls are used for and how to perform some of the operating tasks—things that a new person would need to know about. I filmed the SMEs as they talked about their machine and explained how it worked. After this, I went through the footage and took snapshots to create images (using VLC media player). I then annotated the images using the SMEs descriptions and explanations. It all

came together in a 'New Operator Guide' for each piece of plant.

The footage turned out pretty well especially given it was unscripted (although, no Oscar this year!). As a result, we also decided to burn the footage to disc and give this to the new operator to go with the guide.

All of the guides followed a similar format—Entering and Exiting, Pre-start Checks, Cabin Controls and Operation. The aim was to keep it as simple as possible and easy to follow. Safety was also important, given that the items of plant can be quite dangerous if used incorrectly.

As always, the guides were given back to the SMEs for review and comment. This was then incorporated into the guide. The operators were very passionate about their item of plant, so it was great to talk to them and work with them. The materials will essentially be a support for the new operators to supplement the practice sessions they will receive until they are competent (which will take some time).

Here are a few samples taken from different guides:

In this example, we can see how to enter and exit the vehicle safely. The 'Key Safety Tip' boxes were a suggestion from the Safety Officer who I also sent the guides to for feedback from a safety perspective. The tips are used throughout all of the guides and generally, the information came from the Work Method Statements (WMS) for the particular item of plant.

The pre-start checks are completed each day before operating the piece of plant. I wanted to step the learners through the process. This example comes from the grader and shows how to check the engine area. Where possible, I've tried to orientate the learner to where a small part sits within a larger area. I've done this by magnifying the views of some parts. This way the learner can see where the item sits within the overall picture and then gets some enhanced detail of the part—in this case the isolation switch and a light switch.

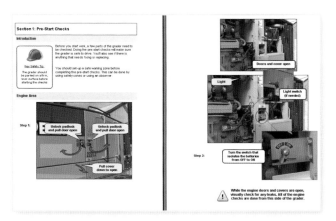

This example shows the cabin controls from one of the trucks. These varied in complexity from machine to machine. For ones that had many controls, I again used the method that showed the whole thing and then enlarged relevant sections which were labelled.

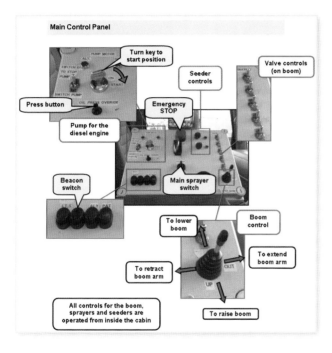

The final part was to show how to operate parts of the machine. This example shows some of the steps to fill a pothole.

The real test will be when the new operators receive the materials once the program starts. I intend to talk with them to gather feedback from their perspective as a learner that I can then incorporate into the materials for future groups.

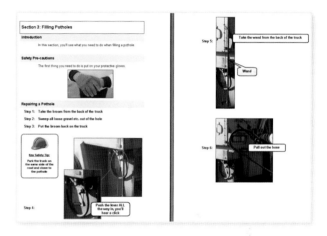

http://learningsnippets.wordpress.com/2013/08/15/showing-my-work-1/

"THIS IS WHAT I DID": DEMOFEST

While work in progress is often interesting, sometimes it makes sense to show work after the fact. Many people already do this by publishing completed presentations to sites like SlideShare or storing them on shared internal spaces.

As part of the annual DevLearn Conference, the eLearning Guild hosts "Demofest," at which learning experience designers are invited to showcase their best work. While there is a competition/award ceremony/prize component, the dozens of entrants value the recognition for their work (which often trickles back to the company) and enjoy discussing it with their peers. Attendees rave about the value of seeing what others have done, with a chance to talk with them about how they did it.

DevLearn DemoFest photo courtesy eLearning Guild.

"THIS IS WHAT I DID": HOW I SOLVED A PROBLEM

Steve Hopkins blogged about how he solved a problem by taking it to a Yammer community.

The Squiggly Line

Business isn't linear anymore. It's squiggly.

08
FEB

Creating smo.ulder.in to export campfire transcripts

ecently, I needed to export a lot of stuff from campfire – about 6 months worth of chats. We used Campfire to host our daily huddle chats whilst we were developing an internal product with Pollenizer recently. They decided to depreciate the service, and I was still keen to get the notes from that for posterity.

However, I was disappointed to find that Campfire didn't support a bulk export function, only the ability to download the notes from each days sessions.

I had a bit of a hunt around, and luckily found Emil's response to a different thread post on the Campfire forums. I've recently turned my hand to trying to learn and use the programming language, Ruby on Rails. But this was still beyond me, so I headed to the Inspire9 Yammering community and asked there if anyone was able to take up the challenge.

Steve Hopkins, Yammer: http://thesquigglyline.com/2011/02/08/creating-smo-ulder-in-to-export-campfire-transcripts/

"THIS IS WHAT I DID, AND WHY": BRUNO WINCK AND UX DESIGN

Bruno Winck is working to create a better experience for users accessing his company's site from their smart phones.

Prototyping the new UX design

Posted on August 21, 2013 by Bruno Winck

I wish to share how I'm designing the new UX for Kneaver.

The goal is to streamline the use of Kneaver, specially on smart phones, according to common scenarios (taking notes in urgence, searching for information while doing something else, reviewing while idle, etc..)

Following advices from Mayra, Andrew and posts from LukeW, I started with the smallest breakpoint : handsets (480*320). I will use responsive design inside a native app.

So what I wish is:

- ⊖ Use paper, pencil, stay away from the computer while designing. Not disturbed, not tempted to lookup existing stuff, not tempted by perfectionism.

- ⊖ Being able to reuse and redo

- ⊖ Explore different aspects, different scenarios, storyboards.

It turns out that even with the lastest HTML5 technology we also end up with only different screens and region changes. So I use cards readily available in commerce, 7.5×12.5, squared. Roughly the size and aspect ratio (1.66 for 1.5) of a small smartphone. I number them in the back. I place them of a sheet of paper, surround them by a large black marker border.

⊖ It's small, I can play with it, bring it outside and try to manipulate it while walking. All cards form a deck and suffice to pick a card to simulate a change of screen.

⊖ Placed in the A4 paper I can add plenty of explanations. Each zone is explained and has a number in a round : this is the priority. if I had to replace, reorder, remove a zone I would go for items with the highest priority. I can write down how I imagine it will be used, thoughts, ideas, critics, alternative I have. A card and a sheet will have parallel lives.

⊖ Placed on a large sheet of paper I can think about all possible transitions. What cause them, what is carried along.

⊖ Later I will reuse it for scenarios.

⊖ I wish to video prototypes as I did for xAPI. Now I realize I could almost do plays. It really opens up a whole world of possibilities.

So now that I have some ideas on how to proceed I will restart from the beginning: doing some interviews on how you learn, stay abreast, apply, retain, capitalize and prepare your knowledge for sharing (email me if you're volonteer for being interviewed!).

This is what it looks like.

The large sheet and my tools:

Detail page:

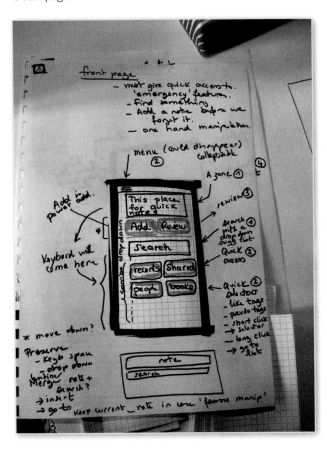

In action low-res prototype. Sufficient to explain it to someone and gather feedbacks.

http://www.kneaver.com/blog/2013/08/prototyping-the-new-ux-design/

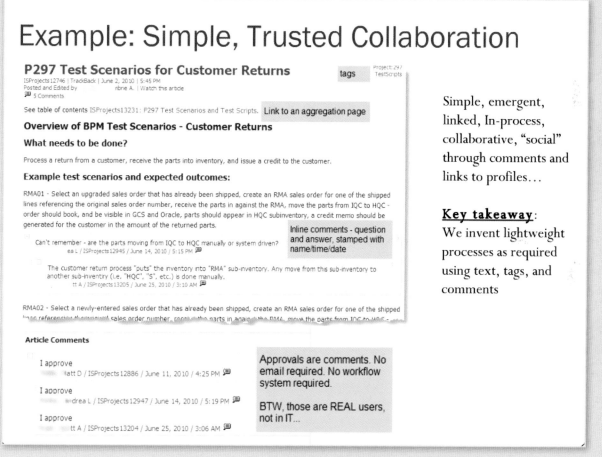

http://nextthingsnext.blogspot.com/2010/07/observable-work-catalyst-2010.html

"THIS IS WHAT I DID": MY PORTFOLIO

Where once upon a time online portfolios were the purview of those with web design skills—or the money to pay for that—new tools make it much easier to create and make public a record of one's skills and accomplishments. Here is an online portfolio from Marianne Abreu, currently a product designer for Samsung.

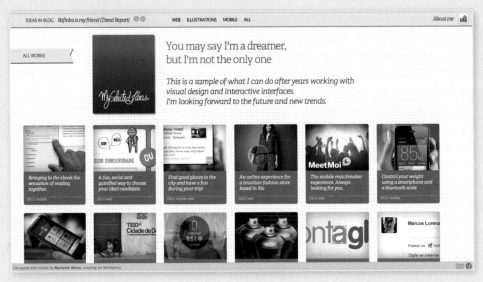

http://marianneabreu.com

"THIS IS WHAT I CAN DO": RÉSUMÉ

Amy Potts went with a different approach to résumé preparation that offers a snapshot of her interests and her work—and her personality.

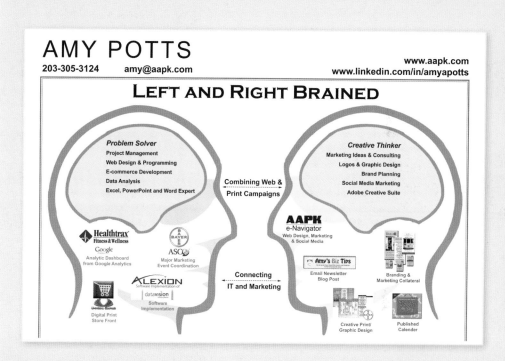

"HERE'S SOMETHING FROM MY WORK I THINK MIGHT BE USEFUL TO OTHERS": DAVID BYRNE

In his 2012 book *How Music Works* musician David Byrne, famous for his work with Talking Heads and more, offers extensive down-to-the-penny detail about his *Grown Back Wards* album, from the risks to the advance to royalties to costs of production, distribution and advertising, down to the amount he pocketed from his work (shockingly little, as it turns out). Why did he offer such an unusual level of self-disclosure? He says:

"I also thought that by being transparent and using my own experience as an example, I could let other musicians see what their options are—and how their decisions might pan out."

~David Byrne

"WHAT ARE YOU WORKING ON RIGHT THIS SECOND?": SNAPSHOTS OF WORKING DAYS

Capturing a snapshot from someone's day—a moment in the trenches—can be illuminating in understanding what people do, who they interact with, and can open the door to opportunity to help or get help.

Employees of Yammer use their own product to "work out loud" as an everyday activity. Yammer's manager of Learning & Development for Yammer Education Services at Microsoft, Allison Michels, regularly asks her team via Yammer, "What are you working on right this second?" Everyone gets a quick snapshot of work in progress, skills being used, problems encountered, and issues at hand. This helps to capture real work in the real moment, not just highlights mentioned at meetings or, as with many workplaces, as lists of activities buried in reports few will see. It also provides a good time to ask for help , which in turn supports a culture of collaboration and sharing. Every now and again the question changes to: "What are three things that have gone really well lately? What are three things that haven't?" This, again, surfaces information often of use to others about how work gets done, not just what is done ("I had the same problem with that vendor"; "I learned that if you call Linda by noon on Thursdays she can usually get a purchase order done the same day. She's slammed on Fridays with her accounting stuff, though"). This builds trust, and openness, and ultimately supports productivity and morale.

"SHOWING WORKFLOW": 2 APPROACHES TO ORGANIZING A CONFERENCE

Many professionals work with event planning meetings and events, some with more success and less panic than others. It's easy to drop a ball when juggling so many. The eLearning Guild and *Training Magazine* both offer several live events a year, with thousands of attendees. Planners must juggle event sites, hotel reservations, complex multiday schedules with dozens of speakers in dozens of slots and dozens of rooms, complicated by presentation equipment needs of each presenter. And snacks. And lunch. And a trade show expo floor. And handouts. And much more. Planning for these events begins literally years ahead with venue and hotel reservations and picks up momentum about a year before the actual event. Seeing how people handle this can be helpful to those facing a large task like this.

Training Magazine's Julie Groshens uses conference-planning software.

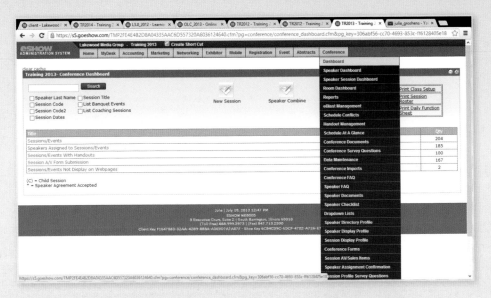

Meanwhile, David Kelly of the eLearning Guild works from a detailed calendar built from sheets of chart paper and Post-it Notes:

Like David, it turns out many people, even heavy users of technology, still often turn to paper and Post-its for planning tasks, a somewhat surprising finding in researching this book.

"SHOWING WORKFLOW": STORYBOARDING MY THESIS

Linda Kirkman, after reading about an author who storyboarded her thesis by laying out visual representations of chapters and ideas on paper, decided to try the same approach with her graduate thesis. She found outlining it with Post-its a useful approach and said talking it aloud to her cat helped her articulate her thoughts. The piece that inspired Kirkman was in turn a reflection on reading about an author who storyboarded novels.

http://patthomson.wordpress.com/2013/03/28/story-boarding-the-thesis-structure/

"SHOWING WORKFLOW": THE EVOLUTION OF A PAINTING

April Barci added 4 photos.
July 4 at 10:57pm · 🌐

Started a new painting a few days back....a few pics from start till now....much much more to go.....but it's cool to see it develop as I go along.... 🙂

Share   1

18 people like this.

Mike Rohde's **The Sketchnote Handbook** (see my sketchnotes of it) focuses on pen-and-paper sketchnoting. I really enjoy digital sketchnoting, although there's a bit more of a barrier to entry in terms of hardware. I've figured out a pretty sweet workflow for live-publishing conference/event sketchnotes so that you can catch people while they're looking at the Twitter hashtag. Mike and I will be talking about digital workflows and tips for one of his podcasts, and I wanted to sketch my thoughts/talking points in preparation.

"SHOWING WORKFLOW": SKETCHNOTING TO SHOW … SKETCHNOTING

An example we've seen earlier is sketchnoter Sacha Chua.

It seems only fitting to close the examples of "This Is How I Do That" by sharing the ways in which two authors approach planning a book.

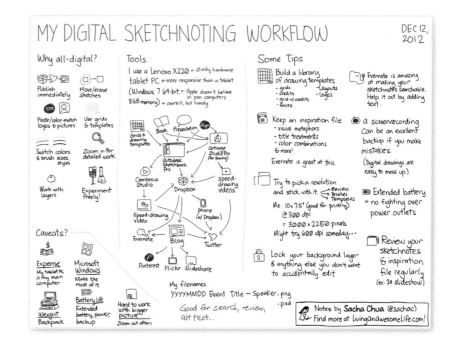

"SHOWING WORKFLOW": TWO APPROACHES TO PLANNING A BOOK

Nancy Duarte, author of the highly visual books *Resonate* and *Slide: Ology*, builds the first draft of her books in PowerPoint.

"SHOWING WORKFLOW": BOOK LAYOUT

Author Jane Bozarth, meantime, gathers ideas first in Evernote, then prints off bits and pictures and big ideas, organizing them on the wall with notes on color-coded Post-its. This helps her see how the items will fall into big buckets of ideas, while being able to move items around lets her try different ways of organizing the content.

The point of all the rapid-fire examples here is not just to show what people share. Or how. Or when. It's that it can be done in so, so many different ways, using so many different tools. Formal. Informal. Professionally reviewed. Freehand. Every item here is of value to someone else. Finding ways to make showing our work part of our daily workflow is a challenge worth meeting.

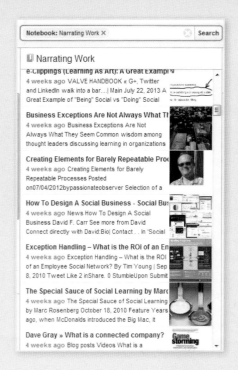

"The point is to extract learning FROM work, not impose more work."

– CHARLES JENNINGS

Learning & Development

WHAT'S L&D'S ROLE?

It's no secret that Learning & Development (L&D, aka "the training department") is often removed from the action: a common criticism is that L&D doesn't know what it's like in the "real world." While ride-alongs and site visits might help, they don't always provide the full picture of how a worker's day is spent and what situations and decision points he or she might encounter. Charles Dhuigg's *Power of Habit* offers the case of Alcoa, an aluminum manufacturer. Despite an intensive companywide concentration on safety, a worker sidestepped protocol to clear a malfunctioning machine part and was killed when the sweeping arm inside a vat restarted. Video recordings showed a number of system failures, including a few that pointed back to inadequate training. What would have been helpful for L&D to know? How could the workers in the area have shown their work?

Helping people show their work can both extend our reach and inform our practice, and in many ways L&D is uniquely positioned for this. We interact with staff at all levels, from novice and new hire to executive, so have enormous potential for influence. Our access here gives us a vantage point in identifying the stronger workers, the ones with skills or knowledge in particular need of capturing. Assuming new roles like online discussion facilitators and community managers position us both to serve as bridges and connectors between people and talent pools and organizational silos and as those who can identify expertise and anecdotes for capture and retelling.

Positioning ourselves as helpers in showing work helps us to support learning in work rather than just learning at work, and helps us get into the spaces between formal training events. It helps learners find and connect with one another, rather than as a one-off interaction between learner and training department. The L&D department actively engaged in helping others show their work will find it a valuable means of formative assessment: How are workers doing? Are they getting it? Are they on track?

WHAT DOES LEARNING LOOK LIKE?

In 2012 teacher Jeffery Heil and professor Valerie Irvine set up a Pinterest board titled "What Does Learning Look Like?" (www. pinterest.com/jheil65/what-does-learning-look-like) As of this writing the board has sixty-two pins. It looks a lot like the one shown here.

Note that NOT ONE picture shows people sitting in chairs listening to someone else talk. There are people working together and talking together. There are people alone doing something: riding a surfboard, building a birdhouse, looking through a microscope. Learning happens when people explore an idea, talk to each other about it, explain their thinking, share what they're doing. Talking about and showing what we're doing helps us learn, and helps others learn.

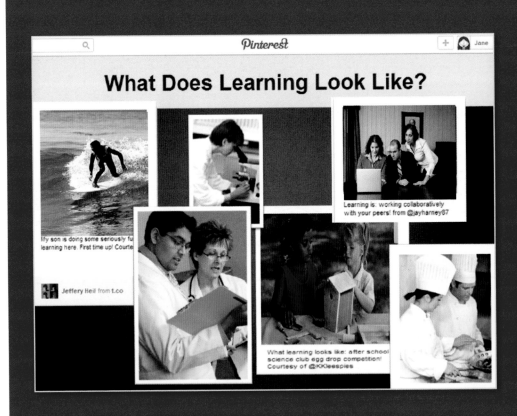

WHAT CAN L&D DO?

Help people capture, publish, and find information

⊖ Offer training in using tools along with any organizational guidelines (on public vs. private sharing, for example). Show examples of how and what others are doing. Don't let this become bigger than it needs to be, though: the best tools won't require a long learning curve.

⊖ Help with idea capture: Take photos, help make videos, teach workers how to use photo editing apps and Windows Movie Maker or iMovie. Show them how to take and edit computer screenshots.

⊖ Help workers make items available: choose platforms and develop processes. Who will share what, where? Online public, online private, in person? Within their unit, team, section, unit, organization? By work area, job class, project, interest, area of expertise? Do they know how to access SharePoint, the wiki, or the LMS? Establish protocols for linking items back to worker profiles or artifacts, for tagging items or otherwise storing/making them retrievable (issues with naming items and versions of items, and tagging them with keywords, bedevils most people trying to find anything anywhere anytime). Think about the structure that makes sense for people and the kind of work: Do you need a wiki by business unit, team, section, project, interest, or expertise?

⊖ Don't forget workers who are not "knowledge workers" and those who aren't strong writers. Give them easy processes and help them with tools that provide for quick sharing via visuals or voice.

FOR EXAMPLE?

Assign a wiki page to each person in the organization who designs presentations. This will likely cross many job categories, units, people, and levels of expertise. Ask them to provide a snapshot of what others do and what they're presenting on. Show them how to upload and link out to a slide sharing tool like SlideShare; teach them how to add a quick voiceover if they want to explain what they're working on or offer notes about the presentation. The wiki pages are editable by those designing the presentations and available for viewing inside the company. Tie this if you like to L&D efforts with "presentation skills" or PowerPoint workshops. At the end of the calendar year hold a "best presentation" contest with prizes for the most articulate, most attractive, most interesting, most fun, and most useful presentations.

FOR EXAMPLE?

The Cheesecake Factory restaurant chain offers its video café to employees via an internal video channel. The company showcases top talent by filming them as they perform their jobs—assembling an architecturally challenging salad, decorating a cheesecake, performing other processes—and makes them available company-wide. A decade ago L&D would have gone to observe the employee, then gone back to the office to make a video themselves. New technology makes capturing video a much easier task, and the age of YouTube has made viewers much more forgiving of less-than-perfect-polished film. This practice helps to recognize talent, surface expertise, connect people with similar interests, and offer teaching aids.

FOR EXAMPLE?

In a previous L&D job, TayloringIt's Craig Taylor planned a series of "video stories" for sharing on the company's internal social platform. Some of the stories he found, or that found him, in his words:

☞ Sales success stories—Interview the top salesperson of the month—what did they do/say/etc. that made them the top salesperson? What made them perform better than others.

☞ Sales horror stories—what went wrong with a sale that they thought was guaranteed?

☞ Thinking and acting differently stories—recording people who were doing something differently. Why? What effect was it having? One particular story centered around a team who were feeling "stale." They decided to take turns to identify a TED talk and distribute it to each team member prior to each team meeting and to use time during the meeting to discuss the content of the video. The upshot of which was that they felt re-energized as a team and several "innovative" new ideas were forthcoming.

I also stumbled upon an interesting story whilst interviewing my former HR director Brett Reid as part of the learner survey I was undertaking. In it he tells a story of conducting a series of coaching sessions with a colleague in Spain, utilizing the FaceTime function on their iPads.

The "takeaway" from the video was to challenge your preconceptions (he had originally been sceptical over how well the sessions would run if they were not face-to-face).

http://tayloringit.com/2013/08/the-ones-that-got-away-video-stories/

FILL NEW ROLES

New tools and approaches bring new shoes to fill: roles like "community manager" and "curator" and "data wrangler" are new to most organizations. There is a natural space here for L&D to help nurture communities like evolving groups of new hires to alumni groups of an organization's leadership academy or a commercial endeavor's training certification program. Workers inundated with information appreciate a good curator, someone who can filter and distribute information from a particular point of view or according to an organization's established practices.

SUPPORT SERENDIPITY

A great deal of what we know, and do, and accomplish, comes about through happenstance. There is a chance encounter, happening across just the right article on the internet, an odd link between events three years apart. L&D practitioners can help to support serendipity by helping to make introductions, make connections, help people find each other. L&D can help find spaces for people to gather—face to face or online—to up the chances that talent can find each other and conversations ignite some sparks. Greg Lindsay, a visiting scholar at New York University who studies interactions in the workplace, says: Most companies are "still really primitive at this. They compress people in the same space, put in a coffee machine and just hope that something good happens." (http://online.wsj.com/article/SB10 00142412788732379810457845508121850 5870.html/.) How can L&D make this better?

L&D NEEDS TO NARRATE WORK, TOO

First: we need to set the example. Too many initiatives have involved the L&D department saying: "Here's the training, now you go perform." We need to be partners and exemplars, not just voyeurs. We need to participate, give and get feedback, and encourage continuous sharing.

LEAD BY EXAMPLE

Introduce tools. Show it can be done. Be the change. Be the positive deviant.

One day during a webinar on "positive deviance" participants started commenting in the chat box about how the conversation reminded them of song lyrics. This was a perfect opportunity to show a tool—and a little-used feature of it—in context as well as a chance to talk about using music as a support for learning. Rather than shut down the conversation, I popped open Spotify, created a collaborative playlist, and invited everyone to add to it.

Later I shared this as a YouTube video: http://youtu.be/rvRfZudhGro

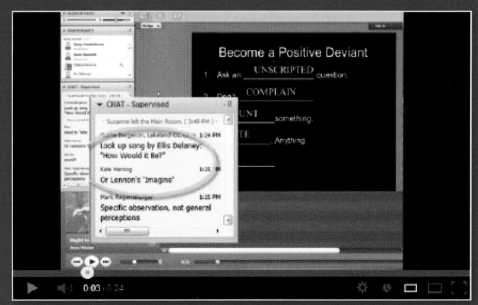

Be the one to make it public. Consultant Trish Uhl travels the world offering prep courses for ASTD's Certified Professional Learning Practitioner exam. She frequently posts what she is doing in class; here are items created by participants in one of her Owl's Ledge CPLP prep workshops.

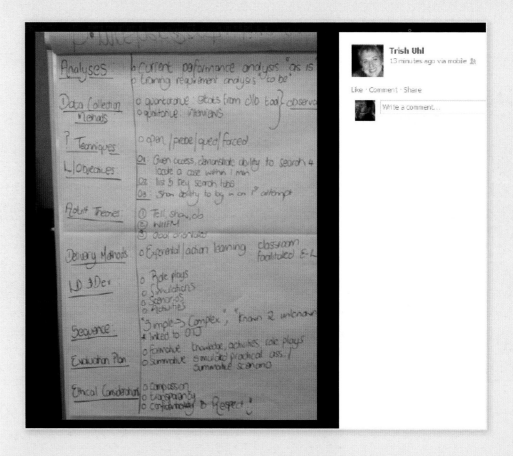

Bonus: this approach can also serve as course marketing and as a way of supporting transfer of new learning back to the job, as it helps others see what happens in the class and helps managers better understand what is covered.

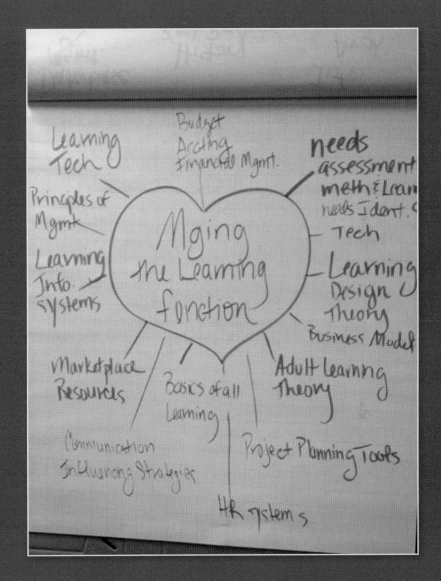

L&D Practitioners: A great way to be sure you are included in and viewed as a part of making work visible and discoverable is to—go first.

HERE'S YOUR CHANCE TO SHOW WHAT L&D CAN DO

Looking over a Twitter conversation among those in L&D, or watching a discussion in an L&D-related LinkedIn group (or talking with our families) reveals a common frustration: People don't really understand what L&D does (or *could* do), or worse, they think designing training experiences is nothing more than putting a lecture together with some slides.

Craig Taylor's experience redesigning a unit's slide deck—described in detail in the "Benefits to Individuals" section—gave him a chance to show his talents as well as offer a small, rare chance to do a bit of teaching about how and why training practitioners make the decisions they do.

Sometimes it makes sense to create a 10-minute standalone tutorial on "How to Create Better Presentations." But sometimes it makes more sense to sit down and help solve one problem, in one real context, for one person who needs that.

SHOWING LEARNING SPAWNS NEW LEARNING

Learning rarely happens in a neat straight line. Gloria Mercer's hand surgery led to learning about cookie making, which in turn spawned an interest in sharing her work, which led to a need to learn about photography and managing a business Facebook page. This piqued her daughter Marlo's interest in cookie making and led her to opening her own business and then to a need to know about web design.

Those in L&D tend to talk about "learning" with a capital "L." But that's not how workers think of it. Learning, for them, is often unintentional and serendipitous, and frequently unconscious. If they see it at all, it's more likely as "solving a problem" or "getting an answer." Helping workers narrate their work can help them become more mindful of learning as it happens, and perhaps more intentional about sharing what they're learning. When Gloria Mercer set out to learn to make cookies she

"Social communities leverage an increasingly expensive asset—people—by allowing them to work out loud, connect with more people, establish trust, and find relevant information and solutions more quickly."

– Rachel Happe

had no idea it would be of interest to so many people, and recognition from others helped her become more focused on documenting and sharing what she was learning—finally culminating in teaching others.

Don't forget the Vanderbilt study described in the "Benefits to Individuals" section, in which researchers found that explaining our thinking to someone else helps us learn. A critical part of the L&D function is helping learners become better learners, and there are few ways more powerful than helping people to show their work.

And finally: For years L&D has wrestled with the challenge of making their work more a process and less an event. This is our chance. Making the process of showing work painless (and if possible, fun) will go a long way toward helping efforts at showing work a positive and probable proposition. There are lots of opportunities for L&D to be part of the effort.

 Melissa Hicks
@seriouspony

Provide support, tools, knowledge, laughs, safety nets, and fun.

💬 View conversation   ↩ Reply   ⟲ Retweet   ★ Favorite   ••• More

Cuba Gooding, Jr., on working on The Butler*: "Whenever I'm working with an advisor it isn't like I ask him questions. I watch him. Because it's something he's doing when he's not advising that I want to steal for the character— the way he holds his chin, his posture, how he undoes his tie."*

Time, August 26, 2013.

Think back over the oddest moment of your day, or the strangest encounter, or the most puzzling problem. What story would you tell your five-year-old when you get home?

How?

This book offers many examples of ways we can show our work. Whatever appeals to you and whatever approaches you wish to take, it's critical that someone—and it might as well be you—be the leader. This book is aimed at readers from all areas of an organization, from frontline workers to CEOs, and at those who don't work within an organization at all. Whatever your place, the key to getting started is to . . . start. Be the first one to go, the one to set the example, the one to lead the effort. This chapter offers tips for managers, trainers, workers, and people just helping each other. Maybe everyone won't follow suit. But a few will. And it will grow from there.

SHIP IT

- In looking for ways to get started, pay attention to things already in place that can be leveraged: internal tools, social tools being used by the marketing and information offices, that kind of thing.

- Locate ambassadors. These are not "champions," rah-rahing about how everyone needs to do this. They are the ones already doing it: they tweet about their work, they upload presentations to SlideShare, they include images in their weekly reports. They are already using tools and demonstrating a willingness to share. Look to them for help and ideas.

- Break old habits and force use of new tools and approaches. For instance, Alcoa's Joe Crumpler and Brian Tullis advise: If you distribute an artifact (file, page, presentation, etc.)—link to it. Do not send the information itself unless it's absolutely necessary. No more email attachments, in other words.

- Encourage one another. Offer "likes" on items or comments when a tool makes that available. Ask questions. Extend conversations where that makes sense.

- Organize around roles, not around the O-chart. Set up spaces and tools so everyone in sales across the organization can communicate with all their colleagues. Or customer service providers. Or trainers. Or people who work with budget processes.

- If you have them in place, work with community managers to connect talent pools, interests, and resources, and to identify areas ripe for showing work.

- Make more things public.

- Instead of asking for just "results" on reports, ask for one line on obstacles encountered and how they were overcome or a description of an unexpected delay and how it was resolved; or mention the person who turned out to be key contact.

- Teach people to create useful profiles, not just job title-degree held. What are their passions? What do they feel they excel at? What is some little-known ability? You never know when you might need someone who speaks Tagalog or knows how to tune a piano.

- Link things—reports, publications, presentations, worksheets—to real people with those useful profiles.

- Workers have to feel that it's worth their while to do this. Learning something from others, getting a solution to a problem, finding expertise when they need it, will encourage them to participate more than will an order to post something every Friday.

- Look for where natural communities exist. All organizations have "unsanctioned" or informal communities, from people who engage in a certain task to those with particular backgrounds or degrees, to others with common work roles.

- Ask, "How did you do that?" and "How did you learn to do that?:" and "Can you show me how to do that?" and "If you did that again next week, what would you do differently?" Learning how Pearl Fryar creates gorgeous, living topiaries does not come from saying, "Please write down what you did this week." Try asking: "What are you working on?" "What problems did you run into?" "What went easily?

What turned out to be more difficult than you thought?" "Where did you have to stop to look for something, or someone?"

- Figure out ways to get it in front of people: Yammer's Allison Michels often asks, midway through a long afternoon, "What are you doing right this second?" and gets fascinating tidbits about processes, projects, and daily challenges and obstacles. Have an autoreminder set up so you'll remember to do it.

- Replace existing activities:

- Instead of meetings, we will _____
  Instead of status updates, we will _____
  When you finish a presentation, _____
  When you complete a sale, _____

- When you _____ (take a break, finish a task, come back from lunch…)

- Once a _____, write down or post a comment or share a photo.

- Start thinking about new roles—some we're still inventing—and who might fill them. The future will include people with roles like Community Managers, Curators, InfoWizards, Data Wranglers, and Connectors.

- Organize around roles instead of silos. Look for existing communities, even unsanctioned ones (every organization is filled with bootleg communities). Work with community managers or those who appear to be influential within communities. Look for natural communities and easy wins: new hires. Alumni of the corporate leadership academy or sales training. Focus on smaller groups. And as you're starting, focus on those who are willing, who will serve as ambassadors for the effort.

- Encourage serendipity. The United States' National Public Radio (US) National has held "Serendipity Days" in which about fifty employees from different departments volunteer to get together to brainstorm about projects. Partly this is to encourage people to "work with groups you wouldn't ordinarily work with through the course of your week," according to NPR's senior director of talent acquisition and innovation. (Source: http://online.wsj.com/article/SB1000142412788732379810457 8455081218505870.html)

- Ask, "How did you do that?" and "How did you learn to do that?" and "Can you show me how to do that?" and "If you did that again next week, what would you do differently?" Then talk about where and how to make that visible/discoverable.

- Look for easy wins: New hires will do as they're asked without saying, "That's not how we've always done it." Set up a site, like a Facebook group or internal wiki, where graduates of the company Leadership Academy can, as part of follow-up coursework, post to their community discussing their successes and areas in which they still struggle.

- Link. Blog contributions should link back to the contributor's profile. Reports of work done by a project team should offer links back to all the team members' profiles. Discussions of using an internal tool should include a link to the tool. Conversations about an item in a policy should include a link to that section. Stop enabling less useful activities, like attachments to email.

- Focus on smaller groups, and focus on reality. Not everyone will be a willing sharer. Not everyone will contribute equally. Focus on those who get on board more quickly and work from there.

THIS SHOULD NOT BE HARD. Whatever you decide to do, it shouldn't require custom platforms, two days of training, and a task force working up an implementation plan.

NAME THINGS

One of the biggest challenges in information management is what to call things. This is compounded by users who do things like rename documents rather than just giving them a new version name. If there is one thing that needs to be formalized it's probably issues around names, tagging, keywords, and folksonomies. Teach that.

As Brian Tullis and Joe Crumpler note in their "Next Things Next" blog: "No matter what Google says, it is important to give search engines some help. You need to be 'discoverable,' and a great route to that is through naming conventions. There is an art to naming files, articles, web pages. Think about your audience and have some discipline to how you 'name' things within your organization without going overboard into taxonomy hell." http://next-thingsnext.blogspot.com/2010/11/tug-2010-observable-workshop-notes.html

PLATFORMS, TEMPLATES, FORMATS

Joe Crumpler, senior manager at a large aluminum manufacturing company:

 Show Your Work 5   ♥ Like 7

"I want to see more from my project team, but I've found starting small is the best way to get people writing. I ask them for the first three items, what I actually want is the full list:

1. Describe the previous day's events (Or describe the current day as you work)

2. Describe potential risk items

3. Telegraph failure and potential misses

4. Describe new action items (things that were not part of the plan)

5. Link to relevant deliverable or changes in scope

6. Comment on questions posed by readers

7. Anticipate what interests a reader

8. Keep the Program Manager informed

It's easy to expand adoption to include the additional concepts. I use a version of the Socratic Method to encourage discussion and help with the adoption of new concepts. Simply asking the right questions will lead people down the path of observable work. For example, when a PM notes a potential miss, I post a question asking what recovery measures are in place and who is responsible for them. The next time the PM makes a post, I often find the information is included. I keep asking questions until the PM learns to narrate the story in a deep and meaningful way. I reinforce the process daily."

—Joe Crumpler http://nextthingsnext.blogspot.com/
2010/11/narrating-your-work.html

Jeroen Sangers uses an ongoing daily-journal process, shown in the next column.

As much as possible, let people use the tools they like best, and let them use public tools if they like. One of the problems with enterprise social networks, as Harold Jarche has pointed out, is "Even with a clear resonating purpose, salaried employees still own nothing on the enterprise social network. Aye, there's the rub." (http://www.jarche.com/2013/05/social-net-works-require-ownership/.) Or if they are already sharing work, recognize that, within the rules or organizational communication policies, they may want to replicate it. Some employees post to the live feed in the company learning management system (LMS) but may choose to repeat the posts on Twitter or on their Facebook pages—or vice versa.

Finally, when working on a big project, I try to communicate **each day** at least these points:

1. What I have done today

2. What I have been unable to do

3. What are the risks I have identified that will affect the project planning

4. What my plans are for tomorrow

During the day I keep a document open where I gradually answer these points. At the end of the day, I just have to publish it.

http://en.blog.zyncro.com/2013/05/16/working-out-loud/

HOW NOT TO DO IT?
DON'T OVERFORMALIZE
OR OVERENGINEER

As Charles Jennings says, the point of showing work is to extract the learning from it, not impose more work on it. The busy knowledge worker or copier repair technician has little time or patience with one more complex, formalized process. Try to think of showing your work as an act of generosity, of helping each other out, not as another onerous task to perform.

NOT THIS,
IN OTHER WORDS:

Think about what is quick and easy and makes sense in the context of work. For the copier tech it may be taking a smart phone photo of a broken part and posting it to a community wiki. For the knowledge worker it may be uploading a finished presentation to a shared site along with a microblog message: "I just uploaded the specs for the Jacobs project . . . ."

Do have some basic ground rules. A couple solid ones? "No anonymous posts or comments" and "when it's evident a conversation needs to be kept between two people, move it to a private channel." Consider what needs to be shared where: some things may only need to be visible to the immediate work team, while others can be placed on a public site. But beware "resistance by delay" behavior, where endless meetings about processes and protocols about showing your work—in the name of making it all perfect—prevent any actual activity. Utilize communication policies already in place, and use the image at right to frame conversations about which items best go in which area.

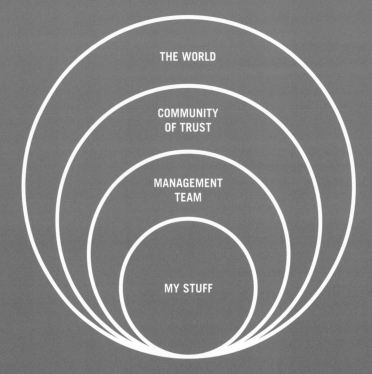

Joe Crumpler http://nextthingsnext.blogspot.com/2010/11/risk-of-exposure-in-observable-work.html

CONSIDER THE VALUE OF MAKING THINGS PUBLIC

While it is natural to worry about letting workers just talk about anything on public forums, this isn't a new problem. After all, the introduction of the telephone presented similar challenges. We have rules about public disclosure and organizational communication policies to guide what can be said where. But avoid the temptation to think of everything as "confidential." You may recall seeing in the "Workers: What's In It For Me" section the example of using Google Docs and Twitter to crowdsource a definition of "professionalism" as part of an organization's code of conduct.

The result:

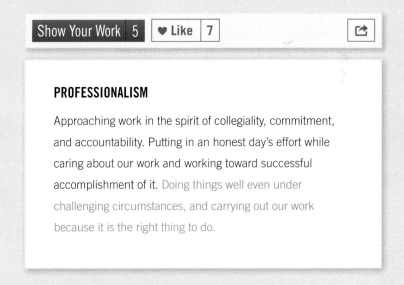

I used this poster as an example of showing my own work in a "Show Your Work" workshop; a participant from Australia used it to create a poster for his workplace kitchen.

Showing work can help to amplify and grow a message, and help tools and ideas find reuse. Consider the nature of conversations: Is there any reason to keep a discussion of the organization's code of conduct secret? It's something that, even if not open to the whole world, would probably serve to generate some conversation between organizations and their customers and suppliers.

And consider: Organizations sometimes seem unaware of who makes up a worker's real network. There's a tendency to view workers in a building, or on a floor, or in a suite interacting with those in the immediate area. But a copier repair technician's network involves other technicians, and the customer who owns the machine, and maybe engineers, and possibly even vendors of auxiliary products like paper or toner. There are legitimate business reasons for some conversations to happen outside the work unit and the organization.

Courtesy of Lee Woodward

"Social communities leverage an increasingly expensive asset—people—by allowing them to work out loud, connect with more people, establish trust, and find relevant information and solutions more quickly," proclaimed Rachel Happe of The Community Roundtable . . . . [who] suggested that human capital investments may still be at odds with technology investments, which are supposed to reduce the burden on knowledge workers."

http://scn.sap.com/community/business-trends/blog/2012/10/09/work-out-loud-screams-sap-radio

TOOLS AND STRATEGIES

Finding the right motivation and medium are critical. Whatever tools are used—from Post-it Notes to complex custom platforms—success depends on making them easy to get to, easy to search, and easy to use. While it may not always be possible, try as much as possible to work with tools people already like using. Some of us are PowerPoint whiz-kids, while others love to shoot quick videos. Some of us are writers—and some of us aren't.

Popular workplace tools for showing work are publishing tools like blogs, collaboration tools like wikis, chat/microblogging and instant messaging products, slide- or presentation-based tools. Sometimes these are used in suites, like SharePoint (internal) or Google Drive (public). There are robust public tools like Facebook and private groups within Facebook. There are robust private tools like Basecamp and Jive.

Choose tools that make sense. If technicians need to offer photos or videos of repairs, where will they go? Will they/how will they be stored? Will they/how will they be tagged or linked? Photos can easily be shared in at least a dozen ways, including sending via text, submitting to a shared private album, uploading to a Facebook group, sharing internally via Yammer, publishing to the world via Twitter, or pinning to a Pinterest board. And most importantly: What are they (or you) already using?

An easy starting place? Shared **bookmarks**. Tools like Diigo and Delicious will let individuals share their own bookmarks relative to a particular topic or interest area; group capabilities allow everyone to share what they're reading, what they found useful, what they are using as resources for presentations or reports. Viewers visit a single URL to get access to all the bookmarked items; those doing the bookmarking can add comments to the things they've chosen to share. A list of items associated with showing work is shown here.

Evernote offers a broader view of this idea, allowing viewers to clip, store, and share beyond just bookmarks to whole articles, single images, and the like.

Showing your work via **presentations** is especially easy for those who are creating presentations anyway. Slide shows developed for public presentations, reports, sales pitches, or training can be shared. The most popular presentation-sharing tool at the moment is SlideShare, which allows quick upload of slides along with options to add audio, allow for comments, and follow those who show their work there.

https://www.diigo.com/user/jbo27712

Show Your Work www.pinterest.com ShowYourWork	13 Sep 13
Show Your Work – Webinar by Jane Bozarth (#sketchnotes) www.tracyparish.ca	13 Sep 13
Next Things Next nextthingsnext.blogspot.com	13 Sep 13
"Working out loud": Your personal content strategy	johnstepper johnstepper.com ShowYourWork	13 Sep 13
Julian Stodd's Learning Blog	A place to explore new ideas in Learning julianstodd.wordpress.com ShowYourWork	13 Sep 13

There are many **canvas** tools available. For small ones—that can be viewed on a computer screen—products like mural.ly allow for individual or collaborative development of online murals that can include easily moved and resized images and text. Users can create and share projects, start discussions around any section of a mural, @Mention others to bring them in or speak directly to them. Changes are tracked. Here's an example of a Mural.ly showing the creative process.

Here's a collaborative mural created in Mural.ly (www.mural.ly) by graduates of a workplace certification program. It serves as their takeaway, a public record of "what we learned."

Those wanting to go large or keep it in a physical space can use traditional whiteboards. Even larger? Ideapaint is whiteboarding paint that will turn whole walls into whiteboards.

VIDEO

Video can be captured now with even inexpensive mobile phones and shared via channels like YouTube, Vimeo, or TeacherTube, which offer varying levels of privacy settings and subscription capability. Items can also be linked to other tools. Video files can be shared directly to sites like Facebook, or sent via text or email (beware here of file sizes and data charges). Depending on the product the videos can be easily enhanced. YouTube, for instance, provides annotation tools and some ability to edit after the fact.

Doctors are now experimenting with wearing **Google Glass** during surgery, which allows students to quite literally see through the surgeon's eyes. You can capture and save video with Glass, or connect the live recording to a **Google Hangout** so viewers can join in real time. There are enormous possibilities for showing an eye-view of activities such as repairs, construction, processes, corrections, and interactions. Glass can also capture still photos.

Tools like "sticky notes" can be used for planning a project or event. Color notes can further mark out specific elements or people responsible.

Planning this book

(Note: there are online "sticky-note" tools, too.)

Mobile devices with cameras are at near-ubiquitous levels, and Pew Internet Research reports that half of all adults online are now sharing and uploading their own images. **Photos** are an excellent way of showing work and are easy to share across many platforms and tools.

Tracy Parish similarly created a sketchnote of a "Show Your Work" session, took a picture of it, and put it on her blog—then tweeted to her followers that she had a new blog post.

By 2014 the marketplace anticipates that the new iSketchnote will ship. It's an iPad cover that will send the drawn image directly to the device, without having to take a photo.

Show Your Work 5   ♥ Like 7   ⬆

This was a fantastic session and if you get a chance to listen to Jane over the coming months speak again on this topic, I highly recommend that you do.

I don't actually think my sketchnotes are improving in the fact that there are still so many words on the page and less images. However, the format really appeals to me. I have always been told that I should have been a doctor because my writing is so messy. The (slightly) haphazard format to taking notes this way, or the freedom of the methodolgy, I think is what makes me keep trying to do it.

Regardless, it's me showing a bit of my work. Not to boast. Not for praise. Just to share what I'm doing. Learn from my own reflection. Help others to see how it possibly can be done, even if it's not the best way to do it. And it's fun.

Kevin Thorn sketches out a new project, then shares a photo on public social channels in the next column.

As discussed elsewhere, low literacy workers, those not comfortable with writing, and those who are just busy may find the need to stop and write down what they're doing too time-consuming or onerous. There are a number of **voice-to-text** tools that can help, and will send voice posts to blogs, wikis, even to Facebook and Twitter. These emerge and evolve all the time so look around to see what's currently available. At the moment they are most reliable with relatively unaccented American voices but are getting better. Take a look at Dragon Dictation, ShoutOut, WordPress's blogging tool's post by voice feature, and iPhone's Siri.

In considering "Which tool is best?" it matters more to ask "What's comfortable and easy to use and fits easily within workflow?"

Kevin Thorn @LearnNuggets   31 Jul

#Storyboard sketches for new project > ow.ly/nuMGg #elearning #sketch

💬 View conversation   ↩ Reply ⤿ Retweet ★ Favorite ••• More

Day #10 - storyboard sketches for new project

REMEMBER TO TURN THE RECORDER ON

Half the trick to showing your work is … remembering to do it. One morning in 2012 tech-guru Gina Schreck wanted to test Skype's still-in-beta ten-way video calling feature. She posted a Tweet asking for help (you can't test ten-way video by yourself, see?) and within a few minutes several other people hopped on the call, the author among them. We learned a lot of things—primarily, that there's a reason things are in beta—but the experience isn't limited to just the few of us. This is of value to people who have a bit more trepidation with tech than Gina, or who don't have a community of people who will jump onto an impromptu call, or who need to show an example of "why we need Skype" to some administrator or IT person at work. Luckily, as we were starting, Gina thought to turn on on her screen recorder. She later made the recording of the experiment available on YouTube. At last check the video had been seen by nearly a thousand viewers.

DRAW A PICTURE

Music has a long oral tradition and is usually a very social experience, with songs handed down and techniques swapped from teacher to student and among musician communities. Check YouTube sometime the number of videos offering help in playing a particular piece on the guitar. Those who've learned (or tied to learn) to read music know that traditional music notation has limitations: you can see how a piece should sound but not necessarily how it should feel. Try listening to ten different recordings of any piece of music and you'll likely hear a good deal of difference, even though the same notes are being played all ten times.

Some composers, sharing the frustration with traditional notation, have chosen to use a graphic approach to music. This drawing by Xenakis, for instance, attempts to show the "shape" of the piece.

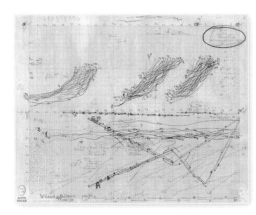

"Study for Terretektorh" (c. 1965-1966), © Fonds Iannis Xenakis, Bibliothèque Nationale de France

In explaining his idea for a new user interface, Bruno Winck drew it, then showed how it would look in context (and then took a picture of it).

http://www.kneaver.com/blog/2013/08/prototyping-the-new-ux-design/

ASK: WHAT WOULD BE USEFUL?

In choosing tools and approaches, Brian Tullis offers an example of what he would need to do in showing work around a particular task:

Make the Process Observable and Linked

There are procedures that describe the capital approval process. There is an official manual for the system in which the requests are entered. I realized that what is missing is a real user guide that tries to answer the question from the perspective of a real person in my department that needs money for a project. Most of those real people look at this situation and have absolutely no idea what to do.

I set out to show:

⊕ Where do I start?

⊕ What kind of data do I need?

⊕ What are real world examples of the inputs, as well as templates to use in a new request?

⊕ Who needs to be notified, and when, and what kind of data will they need?

⊕ Where are examples of completed past requests that I could shamelessly steal? What worked and what did not work?

⊕ What are the real instructions, the "gotchas," both within the approval system and the overall stakeholder communications process?

⊕ What are related processes that this will feed or be affected by this request?

⊕ Who can help me if I get stuck?

What started as a tips and tricks email to a colleague who wanted help in writing his own request evolved into a wiki article. It became a part of our project management resources article, linked to our project methodology's budget instructions.

Formal business process management this is not. Nor is it a 6-sigma black-belted reengineering of a broken process. It's just a few wiki articles and it works well for us."

(Brian Tullis: nextthingsnext.blogspot.com/2012/05/demystifying-complex-process.html)

A case study about encouraging narrating work using Yammer. Within Microsoft. Which owns . . . Yammer.

A 2013 Citeworld.com post offered highlights of an interview with Chris Slemp of Microsoft's IT department. "Our plan for driving adoption includes a mix of broad value proposition messaging such as 'Amplify your influence,' working with teams to replace their distribution lists, and lining up line of business applications for integration with the social platform," he said. "We believe that it's this integration that will drive the biggest culture shift. Employees will just naturally be using social feeds as a part of their jobs in the CRM or engineering tools they use every day."

"Another key to success was not exercising too much control. The power of Yammer is in its ability to enable employees to very quickly self-organize across geographic or organizational boundaries, and around any project or initiative. To realize this benefit, governance is kept to a bare minimum."

Slemp added that Microsoft hasn't been very concerned about quantifying efforts and outcome, but is focused on looking at adoption and the emergence of influencers, and developing use cases to demonstrate value to others in the company.

http://www.citeworld.com/social/21968/microsoft-employees-using-yammer

WORKER CONCERNS

A number of spots in this book offer pointers on dealing with privacy and security concerns, many focused around using existing communication policies and asking, before locking things inside a silo, "Is this really proprietary? Must it be private?"

Employees may have some internal fears about showing their work:

⊖ **Not knowing how or what to show**
Solution: Watch for examples, like the ones in this book. In reflecting on or in conversations about obstacles and successes and roadblocks and workarounds, ask,

"How can we make that more visible? Who else could learn from that?" Create (or join) some role-based communities (HR specialist, sales rep, accountant, nurse, teller, developer, etc.) and listen to what people talk about. They are sharing their work all the time, even though they may not call it that. What do they need? How can you help? What are you doing that would be of use to them? What would you like for them to *narrate?*

⊖ **Needing some help with the tools**
Solutions: 1. Choose good tools. Things should be easy to use, and be accessible without jumping through hoops like additional logins. They should fit well

within the workflow. 2. This is a good opportunity for the training department (L&D) to help people with learning about new tools. But back to point 1: the tools shouldn't have a long learning curve.

⊖ **Fearing what they show won't be useful**
Solution: Encourage commenting and feedback. Ask others to add to the project or conversation. Encourage reuse and be sure to link back to the originator so he or she will see that what he or she is showing is in fact useful.

⊖ **Lack of time**
Solution: Showing work should replace some things currently taking up time, not just eat up more: replace meetings and

activity reports. Take real assessment of how much time in a day is spent on email. Replace it. Ask people to keep a calendar for a week, noting how much time was spent looking for something or someone. Replace that with making work more discoverable.

⊖ **Fear of not getting credit**
Concern: This one is harder as it is tied to organizational culture, which can be wickedly difficult to change. People who work in an environment in which sharing is punished aren't likely to do more of it. People who are in competition with one another for bonuses or workplace awards or other gears in the incentive machine might naturally hoard what they know.

If they're afraid they won't get "credit," then why would they show their work? As blogger John Stepper says: People competing for a slice of a finite pie won't share. Psychology 101 teaches us that all behavior is purposeful. People will do what they are rewarded for, and they will avoid punishment.

⊖ **Fear of being criticized or being made fun of**
Advice: Yammer's Paul Agustin reports this as his own internal hurdle when he first began showing his work, especially when things were in an in-progress rather than finished-polished state. But working in an atmosphere where people must use their

real names to engage, and are expected to behave civilly, taught him to trust his peers.

⊖ **Fear of talking**
Advice: Years ago a colleague came back from a "meeting management" class intent on implementing something called a "Zinger Jar." The idea was that during meetings a glad jar would be placed at the center of the table. Any time someone was sarcastic, or disagreed inappropriately, the group would call "Zinger" and fine the speaker a quarter. In a matter of days nearly every word anyone said was labeled a "Zinger."

Fear of exposing failure

Solution: Work on developing a culture in which failure is tolerated. Consider the alternative: failures that have been hidden can often create bigger headaches later. Recognize that one overreaction to failure can undermine trust and confidence for a long while. Limit conversations where they need to be. Not everyone needs to be privy to every piece of information. Who needs to know about the mistake? Provide spaces where workers feel comfortable, for instance, in writing to the ten people who should know about the mistake, not the entire workforce and all the customers.

Consider: What is the cost of not showing a failure? Teacher Sarah Wessling could have generated a 6-minute video of her perfect lesson plan and her perfect students and their perfect learning from it. Instead she offered 27 minutes showing the lesson crashing and burning, then showing how she fixed it for the next class. This is infinitely more valuable to practitioners and is possible because Wessling has the confidence to show her failings while working in a culture in which one lesson salvaged is not treated like the end of the world.

Some companies have even begun rewarding failure, "Better Ideas Through Failure," *Wall Street Journal*, September 27, 2011, particularly if learning is tied to it. For instance, SurePayroll systems offers an annual cash prize, but only those who try to do a good job, make a mistake, and learn from it are eligible to win. http://online.wsj.com/article/SB100014240529 702040106045765946715725584158.html

Managers: Where/Who is the real obstacle? Employees routinely report that the "Network Administrator" is the one blocking their access to tools. Really? Is your organization letting the network administrator set policy? And consider this, from a "Show Your Work" webinar participant: "If the base media person would cooperate we could record the community of practice meetings." A follow-up conversation revealed that the media person not only refused to help the group but refused to loan equipment and then, when workers offered to use their own equipment, invoked a rule saying workers could not video themselves even for in-house use. Are you aware that your organization's community of practice members want to better document its activities, but your media person is stopping them?

EVALUATING EFFORTS

Microsoft's Chris Slemp says that early efforts at enterprise-wide adoption of Yammer focused more on uptake and emergence of influencers. They recognize that there is no magical algorithm that will help calculate ratio of items shared to outcomes. Those wanting some additional ideas for assessing the value of showing work might be interested in a new conceptual framework developed by Etienne Wenger, Beverly Wenger-Trayner, and Martin deLaat. It looks for ways to identify value across a range of outcomes, from immediate to potential to applied value: why people participate/share in the first place, whether they are making useful connections with others, whether new tools and artifacts are being created and seeing reuse, whether advice is implemented. Moving across the framework to the final two columns, the framework asks for data regarding the effect on personal and organizational performance and, ultimately, whether the organization has begun to work differently.

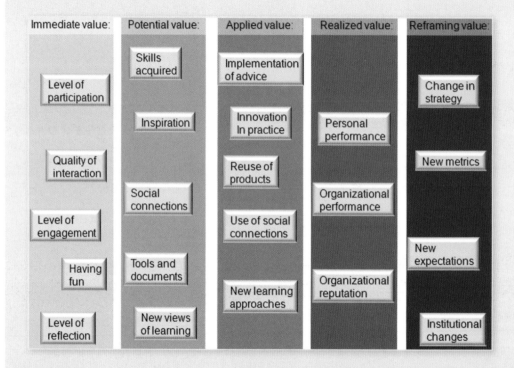

Applying the framework to efforts—which will depend a great deal on workers knowing how to report on what they've shared, with whom, and the results of that, will ultimately show activities looping back on each other as talent and expertise connects in meaningful ways.

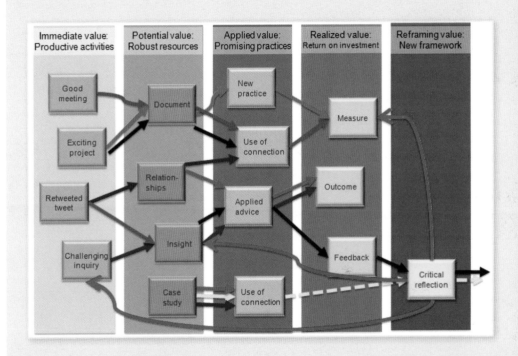

WENGER VALUE-CREATION STORY WORKSHEET

When showing work that involves participation in a network or some collaborative effort, Wenger encourages helping workers be mindful of the value in the experience. Consider submitting this (or asking workers to submit it) instead of requiring whatever activity report is currently in place. Among the tools offered by Wenger et al. is the worksheet on the next page for tracking information across the framework.

For more on the framework, including details on gathering data, see Wenger, Wenger-Trayner, & deLaat,
http://wenger-trayner.com/resources/publications/evaluation-framework/

Typical Cycles	Your Story
Activity Describe a meaningful activity you participated in and your experience of it (a conversation, project, working session, online interaction, etc.)	
Output Describe a specific resource this activity produced for you (an idea, document, other) and why you thought it might be useful	
Application How did you use this resource in your practice? What did it enable that would not have happened otherwise?	
Outcome a. Personal: How did it affect your success or reputation? b. Organizational: Has this contributed to the success of this organization? How?	
New definitions of success Did this change how you think of "success"? How?	

LEADERS NEED TO SHOW THEIR WORK, TOO

If you are the organizational leader, look to the example set by Richard Edelman. And take a look at Paul Levy's "Running a Hospital" blog at http://runningahospital.blogspot.com/. Publish annual plans, and include tangible items people are working on. Even better: publish your thinking. Talk about an especially difficult decision or task. Talk about three things that are going well. Talk about what you had hoped to do when you first stepped into the role, and what reality has taught you.

If you are someone with some control over how visible the activities are within your company or your team, I have some suggestions for you to try immediately:

➲ Post your own personal performance objectives in a public place in your organization. If your employees know what your objectives are, they might get a clue on why you are asking them to do certain things. If they know what you are being held accountable for, they can help make you successful.

➲ If you have a strategy or some sort of annual plan, post it in a public place. That plan should make explicit references to real, tangible efforts being worked on by your team.

➲ When you ask your employees to do something for you, or start a project that involves them, take the time to tell them why. Give them context, discuss linked initiatives, relative priorities, and show them how they are fitting into the big picture.

➲ The next time you create an electronic document at work (or intranet page...), link it to at least one other document or page, to enrich the context of the new piece of information.

➲ The next time you set up a workspace / collaboration site / intranet portal area or even just a file share, give the entire company access to read it. If you can't justify giving the entire company read access, just try for 2x the original number of intended readers—and then let them know that they have access to it.

➲ Explicitly encourage and reward collaborative, visible work.

Crumpler, http://nextthingsnext.blogspot.com/2011/04/whats-vis.html

How does a social COO operate?

Let me show you. Here is a snapshot of my activity on our social news feed today:

- ⊖ Uploaded a follow-up document from our Board meeting and shared with the Board community (13 comments, 7 likes)

- ⊖ Shared monthly reports with Global Leadership Team in the Leadership community (18 comments, 8 likes)

- ⊖ Shared a collection of slide presentations from a recent Microsoft Conference with all employees (22 comments, 11 likes)

- ⊖ Followed up an all-company meeting with details on our new Modern Consulting Practice strategy (10 comments, 33 likes)

- ⊖ Recognized a team member from San Francisco for demonstrating one of our core values (8 comments, 19 likes)

- ⊖ Added my congratulations to our Sydney team who have secured a third contract with a major client (16 comments, 16 likes)

- ⊖ Answered a question by one of our Principal Consultants regarding which former extranet projects would make relevant case studies (24 comments, 9 likes)

- ⊖ Added three new colleagues from New York, Shanghai and Sydney

- ⊖ Followed two new communities

In addition to these actions, I scanned the news feed and noticed a number of activities and updates in regards to project milestones, people and communities, which adds huge value to my day in terms of ambient awareness.

CASE: THE SOCIAL COO

Post from http://nsynergyblog.com/2013/08/26/leveraging-social-tools-to-drive-culture-and-adios-15000-emails/ By Peter Nguyen-Brown, nSynergy COO and Co-founder

WATCH YOUR LANGUAGE

Do you find words like "share" too touchy-feely? Try:

— Making work discoverable

— Making work visible

— Working out loud

— Narrating work

— Showing your work

BE HONEST: ARE YOU READY? WHAT DO YOU NEED TO DO?

A successful organization-wide effort at showing work will depend in large part on the organizational culture. Open Leadership's Charlene Li offers this questionnaire to help you assess readiness and identify areas in need of some tending.

Openness Audit from
Open Leadership

This openness audit comes from the book *Open Leadership* and its purpose is to help you understand just how open you are today. Once you understand how open you are, you can then figure out how open you need to be to achieve your goals. More about "Open Leadership" can be found at http://www.open-leadership.com.

The audit consists of two sections, one around the six elements of information sharing, and the other around the four types of decision making. Conduct an openness audit throughout your organization, compare the results, and gain alignment and definition on how open you are.

INFORMATION SHARING

There are many ways to share information. For each statement about each type of information sharing, rate yourself on a "1" to "5" scale, with "1" being Strongly Disagree and "5" being "Strongly Agree." Just as important, provide examples both internally and externally of each type of information sharing.

Explaining

_____ My organization is disciplined about keeping company information confidential, so that people feel comfortable sharing sensitive information.

_____ The executive team takes the time to explain to employees how decisions are made.

_____ Customers and partners outside the organization

Total _____

Updating

_____ Technology and processes are in place to facilitate sharing and collaboration.

_____ Many executives and employees frequently use social technologies like blogs, microblogging, or collaboration platforms to provide updates.

_____ Shared updates are useful and easily accessible.

Total _____

Conversing

_____ Employees and executives are free to blog and participate publicly in social media as long as they act responsibly.

_____ The organization is committed to hearing from and talking with customers and employees—even when those conversations may be negative in tone.

_____ There is a strong community of customers and partners who help expand the scope of conversation with each other.

Total _____

Open Mic

_____ There are channels through which employees and customers can contribute ideas and content.

_____ The organization actively encourages employees and customers to contribute their ideas and best practices.

_____ Customers and/or partners frequently contribute ideas and suggestions that are adopted by the organization.

Total _____

Crowdsourcing

_____ There is a platform for large groups of people to be able to contribute ideas, innovations, and solutions in an organized way.

_____ There is an appetite to seek out and try new sources of ideas and innovation.

_____ Ideas from outside the organization are frequently incorporated into products, services, and processes.

Total _____

Platforms

_____ Architecture and data platforms are defined and open for widespread access.

_____ Open platforms are seen as a strategic and competitive advantage for the organization, and invested in appropriately.

_____ Many employees, developers, and partners tap open platforms to create new products and experiences for customers.

Total _____

Total Score	Add totals from above _____

Interpreting your score: These scores are not to be used as on absolute scale, but rather as a diagnostic tool for you to understand where your organization is open and where it is not. In particular, understand how you do or don't have the right level of structure, encourage, and exhibit behavior in each area of information sharing.

DECISION MAKING PROCESS

Decisions are made every day in your organization. This part of the audit examines some of the most common decisions that are made in every organization. For each type of decision, identify the decision—making process that is used today, who is involved, what kind of shared information is used to make the decision, and how effective the decision making process is.

To improve effectiveness, you may want to change the decision making process to be more open, but you may also want to consider who is involved or if better information sharing could improve effectiveness as well.

TYPE OF DECISIONS	TYPE OF DECISION MAKING USED *(CENTRALIZED, DEMOCRATIC, CONSENSUS, DISTRIBUTED)*	WHO IS INVOLVED?	WHAT SHARED IN-FORMATION IS USED TO HELP MAKE THE DECISION?	EFFECTIVENESS (SCORE ON A "1" TO "5" SCALE, WITH "1"= NOT EFFECTIVE AT ALL AND "5"= HIGHLY EFFECTIVE
Acquisition				
Partnerships				
Branding/ positioning				
Product development				
Budgeting				
Workflow design				
Hiring				
Others				

WHAT WORKS? LESSONS LEARNED

As mentioned earlier, Hans deZwart conducted an early experiment in narrating work using a microblogging tool with his virtual team (eighteen people total) at Shell. Findings? No one likes the idea of mandatory numbers of posts or comments or deadlines. The posts most people preferred were shorter and timely—as close as possible to the actual performance or event. Participants also preferred posts that were more than just a summation of results, but the thinking that led to them or issues encountered along the way. Apart from being interesting, these were the posts that tended to draw additional conversation and help. One more thing? Posts that revealed something of the author's personality, especially wittiness or fun, and "sharing excitement or disappointment humanizes us, and that can be important in virtual teams, especially in large corporations." http://blog.hansdezwart.info/2011/07/19/reflecting-on-the-narrating-your-work-experiment/

SOME REALITIES

The "legacy information" problem that besets us elsewhere is still present here. Teams change, people come and go, projects are shelved and revisited, people keep renaming the same document. As with websites, it's important for someone to occasionally revisit places and documents, archive old data, and ensure obsolete processes and finished projects are labeled as such. Eventually, this should level out, and the more the work that is visible the closer to accurate everyone's telling will become.

There is also the problem of self-reported data. People exaggerate their accomplishments; they hide mistakes, they take credit. We all need to be heros and often in the retelling our stories put us in that role. But remember, it works both ways: people who are afraid to admit that a project isn't finished, who have been punished for admitting mistakes or failing to manage obstacles, will naturally try to avoid having that happen again.

WHEN?

A question for those just getting started is on the matter of when to show your work. This book offered examples of everything . As with many things, the answer here is, "It depends." While the idea of "narrating" suggests talking as you go, there are some cases when showing a finished product or completed project, or offering a writeup of critical incidents rather than daily diaries, makes sense. Be careful, though, of holding on to something until it's perfect, as more energy ends up going into polishing than into the real bones of the issue. Encourage people to share—and accept without criticism—drafts, sketches rather than polished images, and roughly final ideas.

While it's natural to want to share the perfect, polished, finished product, showing works-in-progress, or at least before-and-after work, can help others understand what is involved in a task. Most things we do do not emerge full blown in one try, but those who don't do what we do often don't fully realize that. Here's an example from designer Kevin Thorn's work in creating characters for an HIV awareness campaign.

Serious Comic— Character Development II
in Design

I can't believe it's been a month and a half since I last posted about this project. It's been a crazy time with traveling to a couple conferences and keeping pace with this development.

My next post was going to be about how to storyboard a serious comic, but a lot has changed in the project since we last talked about character development. With that, new lessons have been learned of which impacted the entire process. This post dives a bit deeper into that process.

Character development for a serious comic is not about randomly selecting a character from an online source. Just like any story, the characters have a personality that you want readers to connect with. It's not just their dialogue, but their other subtle nuances and props that help guide the reader and tell the story.

That all said, our character line-up from my previous post are quite different now. Below is a then and now line-up.

THEN

- -

NOW

Frances　　Carlos　　RJ　　Tiffani　　Stu　　Jan

http://www.learnnuggets.com/2013/03/serious-comic-character-development-ii/

Likewise, a nonfiction book is often about organizing what it likely to be an enormous amount of source material and personal notes down to a final collection (lower right).

In this example, showing work in progress helps to educate the audience about the process. It is also a natural vehicle for showing stakeholders the real status of a project or asking for help when one is in need of getting unstuck.

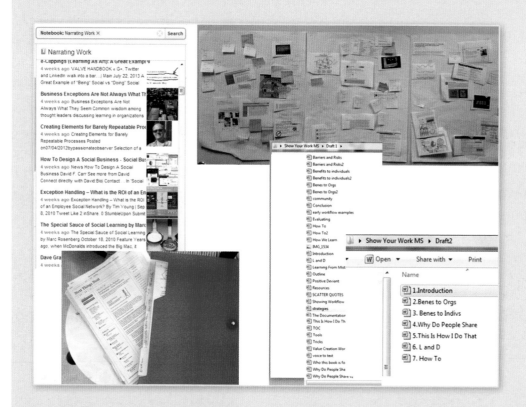

JUST DO IT

OpenText's Kimberly Edwards on the dangers of knowledge hoarding and a reminder that the way to get started is to . . . start:

"Collaborating on content is not new; we have had the ability to do this for years. We all send documents through emails, create wikis together, post documents in team spaces, but what is new is the ease and the velocity in how it can happen when powered by the right tools designed with the right strategies. Now, when I embark on writing a new piece of marketing content or get engaged in a new project I look to my network first to see who can help, who can contribute, and who has had success in this area in the past that I can learn from.

Simply sharing what you are working on as you are getting started, maybe in an activity stream or on Twitter or Facebook or by posting an idea to your ideation app—all of a sudden you are opening a window of opportunity and inviting others to share their thoughts and or ideas. All of sudden you have 10 or more experts at your fingertips helping you to pull together your research and your project suddenly has wings and you are completing your work in half the time and with a renewed perspective (that may be a bit of an exaggeration, but the possibility is there). Imagine if I could write a marketing piece for a new product based on feedback I am getting directly from a beta customer. I am guaranteed that this piece will now have more meaning since I am more aware of the audience. Of course, this sounds easier said than done and much of the concept of 'working out loud' comes with change and we all know that change is hard. Removing the knowledge hoarding is a culture shift and changing culture is an uphill battle, but there are many small steps you can start with. Stop storing files in My Documents and move them to an intranet portal like environment where others can see it and comment upon it and tag it for findability. Look to the community and your network and start discovering where the experts live online."

http://blogs.opentext.com/vca/blog/1.11.647/article/1.26.3010/2012/7/13/
Work_Out_Loud%3A_Stop_Knowledge_Hoarding!

THE END

So the concluding questions: How can we be better about narrating our work? What did we do today that was worth capturing, that might help someone else, that might make something more discoverable in two years?

How can we encourage others to narrate their work? What support or tools would enable that? How about the repair technician who figures out a new, quicker workaround? Or the restaurant chef who develops a new technique? Or the software engineer who . . . ? Or the paralegal who . . . ? What opportunities are we missing? What can we do to help connect the dots across the silos of an organization, or profession, or area of interest?

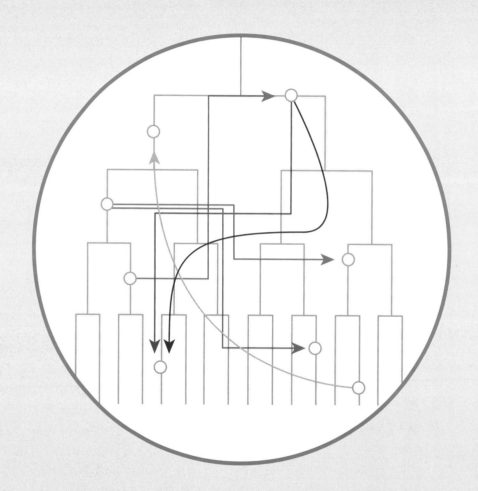

ASK THE RIGHT QUESTIONS

Learning how Pearl Fryar creates gorgeous, living topiaries does not come from saying, "Here's a pen. Please write down what you did this week." We need to stop asking, "Can you tell me what you do?" People have a hard time answering that, and usually just end up listing activities. Instead ask, "What are you working on?" "What problems did you run into?" "What went easily? What turned out to be more difficult than you thought?" "Where did you have to stop to look for something, or someone?" In other words, ask: "How did you do that?" "Can you please show me how to do that?" In other words: we could learn a lot if we did less telling everyone how to do their work and asking them to show us what they do. People talk about their work all the time. Supporting them as they show their work is a great way to help them keep talking.

People talk about their work all the time. How can we make that more visible?

Index

A

Abreu, Marianne, 106
Activity replacements, 138
Agustin, Paul, 37, 159
Alcoa aluminum manufacturer, 119
Ambassadors, 137
Asking questions, 139
Aspen Dental Management, Inc., 93
ASTD's Certified Professional
    Learning Practitioner exam,
    126–127

B

Badaraggo, Joseph, 53
Beach House Cookies, 62
Better (Gawande), 27
"Better Ideas Through Failure" (*Wall
    Street Journal*), 8

Blogs: by Aspen Dental new hires,
    93; Bogush blog on RSA-style
    video project, 66–78; by David
    Sinsky on his self-directed code
    learning project, 89–92; linking
    back to the contributor's profile,
    139; "Next Things Next" (Tullis
    and Crumpler), 140; Paul Levy's
    "Running a Hospital," 166; Steve
    Hopkins on solving a problem
    through a Yammer community,
    101; Terry Block's video on using
    iPad to publish a, 94; UK Ministry
    of Justice's Digital Services, 95;
    voice-to-text tools used on, 153;
    WordPress's blogging tool to create,
    153. *See also* Platforms
Bogush blog on RSA-style video
    project, 66–78
Bogush, Paul, 66

"Book planning workflow", 114–115
Bookmark sharing, 147–148
Bozarth, Jane, 34, 115
Bridget's Everyday Cooking, 6
Brock, Terry, 94
Brown, John Seeley, 2, 4, 7, 51, 53
Burge, Bridget, 6
The Butler (film), 133
Byrne, David, 53, 108

C

Canvas tools, 149
Caramel Apples recipe: expert's
    description of, 6; "Show Your
    Work" approach to writing a, 6–7
Carter, S., 22
Case studies: encouraging narrating
    work using Yammer within
    Microsoft, 157; "Monday Notes,"
    23–27; "the Social COO's" Show
    Your Work, 167
Cheesecake Factory, 122
Chicago Tribune's News Applications
    team, 21
Chua, Sacha, 39, 113
Citeworld.com, 157
Civility issue, 159
Clarity Therapist, 84
CMS, 46
Coaching video, 123
Coastline Cookies, 62, 64
Coastline Cookies site, 65
"Code of Conduct" story: an aside
    on public vs. private contributions
    to, 38; background of the, 34;
    coming up with "professionalism"
    definition by getting help, 35–36;
    Google Doc as being edited by
    a few people, 34; Twitter-based

"Show Your Work" #1rnchat for getting help in, 34

Codifying knowledge, 4

Collaboration: collaborative project presentation, 105; dangers of knowledge hoarding instead of sharing information for, 177. *See also* Getting help; Knowledge sharing

Common Core standards, 17

Communication: how Show Your Work overcomes traps of traditional, 14; "Monday Notes" case study on organizational, 23–26; new ways at Yammer of working and, 37; priority over information, 9; Tayloristic views of workplace, 16. See also Conversations; Dialogue

Communities of practice: cookie-making knowledge sharing example of, 62; knowledge embedded within social capital of, 52; knowledge sharing within, 53; look for naturally-forming, 138; "network administrator" barrier to Show Your Work by, 161; organizing around roles and, 139; spinoff learning shared with, 65. *See also Social* communities

Complications (Gawande), 45

Conference-planning software, 110

Connect Consulting, 16

Connecting the dots, 3

Connecting with remote staff, 22

Constant, D., 54

Consultant work sharing, 84

Conversations: encouraging others to Show Your Work during, 137; knowledge sharing through, 52; on learning from mistakes, 16–19; priority over tools, 9; Show Your Work as creating dialogue and, 33; Socratic Method to encourage, 141; Twitter-based L&D, 128. *See also* Communication; Dialogue

Credibility establishment, 31

Credit/attribution, 159

Crowdsourcing: Open Leadership's openness audit on, 171; for professionalism definition, 35–36, 145

The Crucible, 16

Crumpler, Joe: collaborative project presentation by, 105; on linking in order to distribute an artifact, 137; "Next Things Next" blog by, 140; on purpose in work as intrinsic motivation, 22; on Show Your Work platforms, templates, formats, 141; on value of naming conventions, 140

Customer service improvement, 21

D

Daily-journal format, 142

Debus, Kurt, 23

Decision making openness audit, 171–172

deLaat, Martin, 162, 164

Delicious, 147

"Demofest" (eLearning Guild), 100

Designing: of a mobile app, 82–83; visual choices for, 85

DevLearn conferences: Craig Taylor's recaps on sessions attended at, 87; eLearning Guild's "Demofest" at the, 100

deZwart, Hans, 173

Dhuigg, Charles, 119

Dialogue: Show Your Work as creating, 33; Twitter "Show Your Work" #1rnchat (June 27, 2013), 33. *See also Communication; Conversations*

Diijo, 147

Disaster prevention/continue the flow, 22

The documentation problem, 4

Dragon Dictation, 153

Duarte, Nancy, 114

Duguid, P., 4, 7, 51, 53

E

Edelman PR, 21

Edelman, Richard, 21, 47, 166

Edwards, Kimberly, 177

eLearning Guild: David Kelly's approach to organizing conferences at, 110; "Demofest" of, 100

eLearning knowledge sharing, 61

"Emotional communion," 54

Employee morale enhancement, 22

Engelen, Lucien, 60

Evernote notebook sharing, 39, 148

Evolution of a painting, 112

Expert knowledge: definition of, 52; sharing of, 54–55; of subject matter expert (SME), 97

Expertise establishment, 31

Explicit knowledge, 4

F

Facebook: designing a mobile app shared through, 82–83; Gloria Mercer's cookie-making sharing on, 62, 128; Gloria Mercer's posting on her mistake, 19; setting up a group for workers on, 139; sharing videos on, 150; as Show Your Work platform, 142; Show Your Work tools on, 147; voice-to-text tools used on, 153; when it is appropriate to share on, 8. *See also* Platforms

Failure: fear of exposing, 160; organizational culture that tolerates, 160. *See also* Mistakes

Faraj, S., 38, 53

Fears: of criticism, 159; of exposing failure, 160; of talking in meetings, 159

Formats, 141–142

Franklin, Benjamin, 67

Fryar, Pearl, 41, 59, 138, 179

G

Gawande, Atul, 27, 45

Germuska, Joe, 46

Getting credit, 159

Getting help: an aside on public vs. private contributions to, 38; "Code of Conduct" story on, 34–36; coming up with "professionalism" definition by, 35–36; Google Doc after being edited by a few people, 34; new ways at Yammer, 37; Twitter-based "Show Your Work" #1rnchat for, 34. *See also* Collaboration

Gooding, Cuba, Jr., 133
Google Docs, 34, 145
Google Drive, 147
Google Glass, 60
Google search engine, 140
Government agency, 95
Groshens, Julie, 110
Groskopf, Chistopher, 21
Ground rules for Show Your Work, 144
Grown Back Wards album (Byrne), 108
Guthridge, Liz, 16, 52
Guyan, Matt, 96–99

H

Hagel, John, 2
Happe, Rachel, 129
Healthy conflict, 24–25
Heil, Jeffery, 120
Hicks, Melissa, 131
HIV awareness campaign, 174–175
Hopkins, Steve, 55, 101
How Music Works (Byrne), 53, 108

I

Implicit knowledge, 4
Information: the documentation problem of codifying knowledge and, 4; how L&D can capture, publish, and find, 121–123; how social communities can leverage, 129–130; "legacy information" problem of, 173; linking to artifact in order to distribute, 137; priority of communication over, 9; problem

of self-reported, 173; problem of undersharing, 16; proprietary, 8; the silo problem of accessing, 2, 178; why Show Your Work isn't all about sharing, 9. *See also* Knowledge
Information management: balancing how much to strip out the extraneous, 7; what to name things, 140
Information maps: comparing "expert" versus "Show Your Work," 6–7; don't strip out the landmarks from your, 7
Information sharing openness audit, 169–171
Instagram, 7
International Women's Day, 79
iPads: blogging published through, 94; using FaceTime function on, 123
iPhone's Siri, 153
Irvine, Valerie, 120
iSketchnote, 152
"It Is What One Does: Why People Participate and Help Others in electronic Communities of Practice" (Wasko & Faraj), 53

J

Jarche, Harold, 4, 142
Jennings, Charles, 117, 143
Journal of Experimental Child Psychology, 40

K

Kelly, David, 33, 110
Kiesler, S., 54

Kirkman, Linda, 43, 111
Kneaver, 102
Knowledge: comparing amateur and experienced, 92; continuum of explicit and implicit, 4; distortion of detaching practice from, 53; the documentation problem of codifying, 4; don't overformalize or overengineer, 143; viewed as discrete bits of data, 51, 52; viewed as embedded in communities and shared, 52; viewed as residing in "experts," 52, 54–55, 97. *See also* Information; Learning
Knowledge hoarding, 177
Knowledge management (KM), 5
Knowledge sharing: benefits of, 53; blog on self-directed code learning project for, 89–92; caring and desire to help motivation of, 55; on collaborative project presentation, 105; on consultant work, 84; of a creative resume preparation, 107; dangers of knowledge hoarding instead of, 177; David Byrne on his music career experience, 108; on designing a mobile app, 82–83; on eLearning Guild's "Demofest," 100; "emotional communion" of expert, 54–55; Gloria Mercer's cookie-making videos for, 62–65, 128; Google Glass as tool for, 60; on learning while attending a conference, 87; on Médicins Sans Frontiès (MSF)/Doctors Without Borders, 79–81; "Mission: Turfgrass" online course for, 61; "need-to-know" basis

of, 16, 52; as the new saving of knowledge practice, 55; an online portfolio, 106; openness audit on organizational culture on, 169–171; on problem solving through a Yammer community, 101; on publishing a blog from iPad, 94; of spinoff learning, 65; of takeaway from a webinar session, 88; through habits, routines, language and stories, 52; UK Ministry of Justice's Digital Services blog for, 95; on UX design prototyping, 102–105; Yammer employees sharing snapshots of their working days, 109; Yammer overview of product development choices, 86. *See also* Collaboration; Learning; Show Your Work; Workflow
Knowledge workers, 6, 121

L

Lanius, Roger, 23
Leaders: case study on social COO's Show Your Work, 167; Show Your Work by, 166; Show Your Work to reduce space between workforce and, 21
Leadership Academy, 139
Learning: David Sinsky's blog on his self-directed code learning project, 89–92; extracting from work, 117; from your mistakes, 16–19, 160; Gloria Mercer's cookie-making sharing on her, 62–65; how explaining your thinking helps with, 40, 128, 130; how teaching

others improves your, 41; sharing experience of conference, 87; spinoff, 65; "What Does Learning Look Like?" (Heil and Irvine) on, 120. *See also* Knowledge; Knowledge sharing

Learning & Development (L&D): common criticisms of, 119; examples of, 121–123; fill new role by using, 124; how it can help capture, publish, and find information, 121; how showing learning spawns new learning, 128–131; leading by example, 125–127; making L&D work more of a process and less of an event, 131; narrating work of, 124, 131; Owl's Ledge CPLP prep workshops, 126–127; showing what it can do, 128; support serendipity by using, 124, 139; workplace learning role of, 119. *See also* Training

"Learning from Explaining" (Rittle-Johnson, Saylor, & Swygert), 40

Learning Management System (LMS), 142

Learning Solutions Magazine, 62

Leffler, Nick, 114

"Legacy information" problem, 173

Levy, Paul, 166

Li, Charlene, 169

"Likes," 137

LinkedIn, 8

Linking: distribute an artifact by, 137; to people with useful profiles, 138; Show Your Work by making process observable and, 156

Lowe's "Open Leadership" initiative, 22

M

A Man Named Pearl (documentary), 59

Maps. See Information maps

Marshall Space Flight Center (MSFC), 23–27

Matthews, Heidi, 88

Médicins Sans Frontiès (MSF)/Doctors Without Borders, 79–81

Meetings: replacing existing activities like, 138; "resistance by delay" behavior driving, 144; "Zinger Jar" story and fear of talking during, 159

Mercer, Gloria, 19, 62–65, 128, 130

Michels, Allison, 86, 109, 138

Microsoft, 157

Mike (neighborhood handyman), 2

"Mission: Turfgrass" online course, 61

Mistakes: Gloria Mercer's Facebook posting on her, 19; learning from, 16–19; Post-Mortem Race to the EDGE! Game on, 18; Sarah Brown Wessling's experience with sharing her, 16–17, 160. *See also* Failure

Mobile app designing, 82–83

"Monday Notes" case study, 23–27

Mural.ly, 149

Music recording videos, 154

N

Naming conventions, 140

Narrating work out loud, 43, 55, 177

National Public Radio (NPR), 46, 139

"Need-to-know basis," 16, 52

New York Times, 21

Nguyen-Brown, Peter, 167

O

"Open Leadership" initiative (Lowe's), 22

Open Leadership's openness audit, 169–172

OpenText, 177

Organization, Show Your Work timing for getting started, 174

Organizational benefits: additional Show Your Work, 22; better customer service, 21; improving public perception and awareness, 20; increased efficiencies, 13; learning from mistakes, 16–19; "Monday Notes" case study on communication, 23–27; of observable work, 15; overcoming traps of traditional communication, 14; preserving institutional knowledge, 20; reducing space between leaders and others, 21

Organizational culture: concerns over not getting credit issue of, 159; openness audit for Show Your Work readiness of your, 169–172; removing knowledge hoarding from your, 177; toleration of failure in, 160

Organizations: evaluating Show Your Work efforts of, 162–163; knowledge views as embedded in community of, 52; "legacy information" problem of, 173; Show Your Work benefits to, 13–27; Show Your Work lessons learned by, 173; social capital residing in relationships within, 52

Organizing conference workflows, 110

Owl's Ledge CPLP prep workshops, 126–127

P

"Paid Media–A Change of Heart" (Edelman post), 21

Painting workflow, 112

Parish, Tracy, 33, 152

Partovi, Matthew, 55

Patel, Sameer, 32

Paying it forward, 46

Pegg, Anne Marie, 79

Performance improvement: as individual worker benefit, 32; as organizational benefit, 13

Photos: sharing, 147; Show Your Work using, 152

Pinterest: Professionalism webinar placed on, 36, 146; as Show Your Work tool, 147; "What Does Learning Look Like?" (Heil and Irvine), 120

Platforms: iPads, 94, 123; Open Leadership's openness audit on, 171; overview of Show Your Work, 141–142; photo sharing, 147, 152; Pinterest, 36, 120, 146, 147; portfolios, 39, 106; TED talks, 122; webinars, 36, 125, 146, 161; wikis, 121, 153. *See also* Blogs; Facebook; Twitter; Videos; YouTube

PLN (personal Learning network) [Twitter-based], 34

Portfolios: Marianne Abreu sharing his online, 106; replacing your resume with a, 39

Post-Mortem Race to the EDGE! Game, 18
Potts, Amy, 107
Power of Habit (Dhuigg), 119
Power play information, 16
Poynter.Org, 46
Practice: distortion of knowledge that is detached from, 53; how reflection improves, 41–45; how teaching others improves, 41
Presentations: collaborative project, 105; Show Your Work via, 148
Problem solving: ask others how they went about, 138; "Code of Conduct" story on getting help for, 34–38; sharing knowledge on successful, 101
Product development decisions, 86
Professionalism: an aside on public vs. private contributions to definition of, 38; crowdsourcing a definition of, 35–36, 145; getting help to come up with definition of, 35–36; Pinterest of webinar about, 36, 146
Profiles: linking blogs back to the contributor's, 139; linking information to real people with useful, 138; teach people to create useful, 138
Proprietary information, 8
ProPublica, 21
Public: "Code of Conduct" story and contributions from the, 38; considering the value of making things, 145–146; how Show Your Work can improve perception by the, 20; making more things, 137

R

Raising your profile, 32
Recruitment: David Sinsky's blogs on self-learning used for, 89–92; how Showing Your Work helps support, 22
Reflective practice: challenges of engaging in, 41; description and benefits of, 45; RSA Animate style video project blog on "things I wish I did," 77–78; student nurse's example of, 41; three exercises on, 43–44; tips for successful, 42
Reflective practice exercises: 1: answering basic questions on task, 43; 2: talking it through out loud, 43; 3: printable template, 44
Reid, Brett, 123
Relief operator training: "Key Safety Tip" boxes used as part of, 98; Matt Guyan's project on, 97–99; SME (subject matter expert) role in, 97; Work Method Statements (WMS) used in, 98
Remote staff connections, 22
Replacing exciting activities, 138
Reports: on obstacles and how they were overcome, 137; Wenger Value-Creation Story Worksheet used in place of, 164–165
ReShape, 60
"Resistance by delay" behavior, 144
Resonate (Duarte), 114
Resumes: Amy Potts' unique approach to her, 107; creating a portfolio to replace your, 39

Reyes, Mig, 31, 85
Rittle-Johnson, B., 40
Rohde, Mike, 113
Roles: L&D for filling new, 124; L&D workplace learning, 119; organizing around, 139; SME (subject matter expert) training, 97; start thinking about new organizational, 139
Rowe, M., 6
RSA Animate style video project blog: day five-write the scripts, 74–75; day four-record the videos, 72–73; day one-directions, 68–69; day six-record the narration, 75–77; day three-dress rehearsal...sort of, 70–71; day two-drawings, 70; description and getting started, 66–68; on practice day, 72; reflections on things I wish I did..., 77–78
"Running a Hospital" blog (Levy), 166

S

Safety issues: Alcoa aluminum manufacturer case of, 119; training relief operators and, 97, 98
Samsung, 106
Sangers, Jeroen, 13, 142
SAP, 32
Saylor, M., 40
Schematic or process plan (SOP), 2
Schreck, Gina, 154
Self-reported data problem, 173
Serendipity, 124, 139
Serious Comic–Character Development II, 174–175

Shared bookmarks, 147–148
SharePoint, 147
Shell, 173
ShoutOut, 153
Show Your Work: ask the right questions to encourage others to, 179; the documentation problem solved by, 4; encouraging others to, 178; evaluating efforts for, 162–163; evaluating organizational efforts toward, 162–163; examining the different approaches to, 1; ground rules for, 144; issues to consider for, 5; knowing when it is appropriate to share, 8; leadership example for use of, 166–168; lessons learned on, 173; long tradition of, 5; make the process observable and linked, 156; "network administrator" barrier to, 161; Open Leadership's openness audit for, 169–172; showing work in progress, 176; what to name things challenge, 140; when to start to, 174; why it isn't all about "information," 9; worker concerns about, 158–161. *See also* Knowledge sharing; Work
"Show Your Work" #1rnchat (June 27, 2013), 33
Show Your Work approaches: consider the value of making things public, 145–146; don't make it too hard, 139; don't overformalize or overengineer, 143; ground rules for, 144; overview of platforms, templates, and formats, 141–142; ship it, 137–139; simplifying a

complex story down for a five year old, 135; tips for effective, 168; Wenger Value-Creation Story Worksheet, 164–165

Show Your Work benefits: the documentation problem solution, 4; for individual workers, 30–47; organizational, 13–26; solving the silo problem, 2, 178; for teams, 13–14, 22

Show Your Work tools & strategies: ask the right questions, 179; case study on encouraging narrating work using Yammer, 157; draw a picture, 154–155; issues and types of tools to consider for, 147–149; leadership example for Show Your Work, 166–168; make the process observable and linked, 156; remember to turn on the recorder, 154; videos, 59, 62–78, 122, 123, 128, 130, 150–153; Wenger value-creation story worksheet, 164–165

Sierra, Kathy, 85

The silo problem, 2, 178

Sinsky, David, 89–92

"6 AM" blog (Richard Edelman), 21

"6 Reasons Journalists Should Show Your Work While Learning" (Thompson), 46

Sketchnoting, 113, 152–153

The Sketnote Handbook (Rohde), 113

Skype's recording experiment, 154

Slemp, Chris, 157, 162

Slide: Ology (Duarte), 114

SlideShare, 55, 100, 121, 137

Snapshots of working days, 109

Social capital, 52

Social communities: how they leverage information, 129–130; leveraging people as assets, 147. See also Communities of practice

Social COO case study, 167

Socratic Method, 141

Sproull, L., 54

Stepper, John, 1, 159

"Sticky notes" tools, 151

Storyboard sketches, 153

Storyboarding a thesis, 111

Storytelling, 135

Stroh, J., 8

"Study for Terretektorh" (Xenakis), 154

Suarez, Luis, 37

Subject matter expert (SME), 97

Sugarcoating information, 16

Supporting serendipity, 124, 139

SurePayroll, 160

Swygert, K., 40

T

Talking Heads, 108

Taylor, Craig, 32, 87, 122, 128

TayloringIt's "video stories," 122

TeacherTube, 150

Teaching: how writing a blog can improve your, 45; learning benefits of, 41; sharing lessons learned from mistakes in, 16–17

Teaching Channel site: screenshot showing interface of, 17; sharing lessons learned from mistakes on, 16

Team benefits: connecting with remote or scattered members, 22; increased efficiency of, 13; overcoming traditional communication traps, 14

TED talks, 122

Templates, 141–142

Thesis storyboard, 111

37 Signals, 31, 85

Thompson, Matt, 46

Thorn, Kevin, 61, 82, 153, 174–175

3M, 73

Time magazine, 133

Tolerating failure, 160

Topiary gardening YouTube videos, 59

Toronto Wildlife Centre, 20

Training: Matt Guyan's project for relief operator, 97–99; SME (subject matter expert) role in, 97. See also Learning & Development (L&D)

Training Magazine, 110

Tullis, Brian: on benefits of observable work, 15; collaborative project presentation by, 105; on connecting the dots with Show Your Work, 3; "Next Things Next" blog by, 140; on purpose in work as intrinsic motivation, 22; on showing work around a particular task, 156; on value of naming conventions, 140

Twitter: crowdsourcing by using, 145; getting help from PLN (personal learning network) on, 34; Heidi Matthews' sharing her takeaway from webinar using,

88; L&D conversations held on, 128; Médicins Sans Frontiès (MSF)/Doctors Without Borders updates through, 79–81; sharing information through, 8; "Show Your Work" #1rnchat (June 27, 2013) on, 33; as Show Your Work platform, 142, 147; UK Ministry of Justice's Digital Services blog and use of, 95; voice-to-text tools used on, 153. See also Platforms

U

Uhl, Trish, 126

UK Ministry of Justice's Digital Services blog, 95

U.S. National Teacher of the Year, 16

UX design prototyping, 102–105

V

Vanderbilt University study, 40, 130

Videos: Bogush blog on RSA Animate style video project, 66–78; Gloria Mercer's cookie-making, 62–65; on iPad FaceTime function used for coaching, 123, 128, 130; music recordings, 154; Pearl Fryar's topiary teaching, 59; as Show Your Work tool, 150–153; TayloringIt's "video stories," 122. See also Platforms

Vimeo, 150

Visual design choices, 85

Voice-to-text tools, 153

von Braun, Wernher, 23, 25, 26

W

Wall Street Journal, 8
Washington Post, 21
Wasko, M., 38, 53
Webinars: L&D "positive deviance," 125; "network administrator" barrier to Show Your Work, 161; Pinterest of "professionalism," 36, 146
Wenger, Etienne, 162, 164
Wenger-Trayner, Beverly, 162, 164
Wenger Value-Creation Story Worksheet, 164–165
Wessling, Sarah Brown, 16–17, 160
"What Does Learning Look Like?" (Heil and Irvine), 120
Wikis: Show Your Work posted on, 121; voice-to-text tools used on, 153
Winck, Bruno, 102–105, 155
Woodruff, Steve, 84
Woodward, Lee, 36
WordPress, 153
Work: ask the right questions about people's, 179; benefits of observable, 15; extracting learning from, 117; Learning & Development (L&D) used to narrate, 124; narrating L&D, 124, 131; problem of undersharing your, 16. *See also* Show Your Work
Worker benefits: creating dialogue, 33; establishing credibility and expertise, 31; explaining your thinking helps you learn, 40; getting help and saving time by not reinventing the wheel, 34–37; improving performance, 32; paying it forward, 46; raising your profile, 32; reflection improves practice, 41–45; replacing resume with something more meaningful, 39; using Show Your Work as part of your workflow for increased, 47; student nurse's comments on, 41; teaching others improves practice, 41
Workers: ask the right questions about their work, 179; becoming aware of their real network, 146; creating useful profiles, 138; encouraging them to Show Your Work, 178; evaluating Show Your Work efforts by, 162–163; knowledge sharing among, 54–55; profiles of, 138, 139; setting up a Facebook group or wiki for, 139; Show Your Work benefits to, 31–45; Show Your Work concerns by, 158–161
Workflow: designing a mobile app, 82–83; for evolution of a painting, 112; sketchnoting, 113; storyboarding my thesis, 111; two approaches to organizing a conference, 110; two approaches to planning a book, 114–115. *See also* Knowledge sharing
Workforce: connecting with remote or scattered, 22; how Show Your Work benefits the entire, 6–7; problem of undersharing in the, 16; remembering to focus on other than knowledge workers of the, 6, 121; Show Your Work to reduce space between leaders and other, 21; social capital of relationships formed in the, 52
Working out loud, 43, 55, 177
Workplace: handling proprietary information of the, 8; Tayloristic views of communicating in the, 16; variety of Show Your Work applications at the, 9; where to share Show Your Work approach at the, 8; Yammer employees sharing snapshots of their working days and, 109

X

Xenakis, Fonds Iannis, 154

Y

Yammer: case study on encouraging narrating work using, 157; employees sharing snapshots of their working days at, 109; evaluating efforts for emergence of influencers at, 162–163; new ways of working and communicating at, 37; as Show Your Work tool, 147; video on product development decisions, 86; working out loud practice at, 55
Yammer community, 101
Yipit, 92
YouTube: benefits of sharing by Showing Your Work on, 2; editing tools available on, 150; Gloria Mercer's cookie-making videos on, 62–65, 128, 130; knowledge sharing through, 55, 59; L&D "positive deviance" webinar on, 125; less-than-perfect-polished videos on, 122; music recording videos, 154; Pearl Fryar's topiary teaching videos on, 59; as Show Your Work tool, 150–153; Skype's recording experiment posted on, 154; when it isn't appropriate to Show Your Work on, 8. *See also* Platforms

Z

ZenCap, 89
"Zinger Jar," 159
Zoller, Jeffrey, 42